SUPERNATURAL

SUPERNATURAL

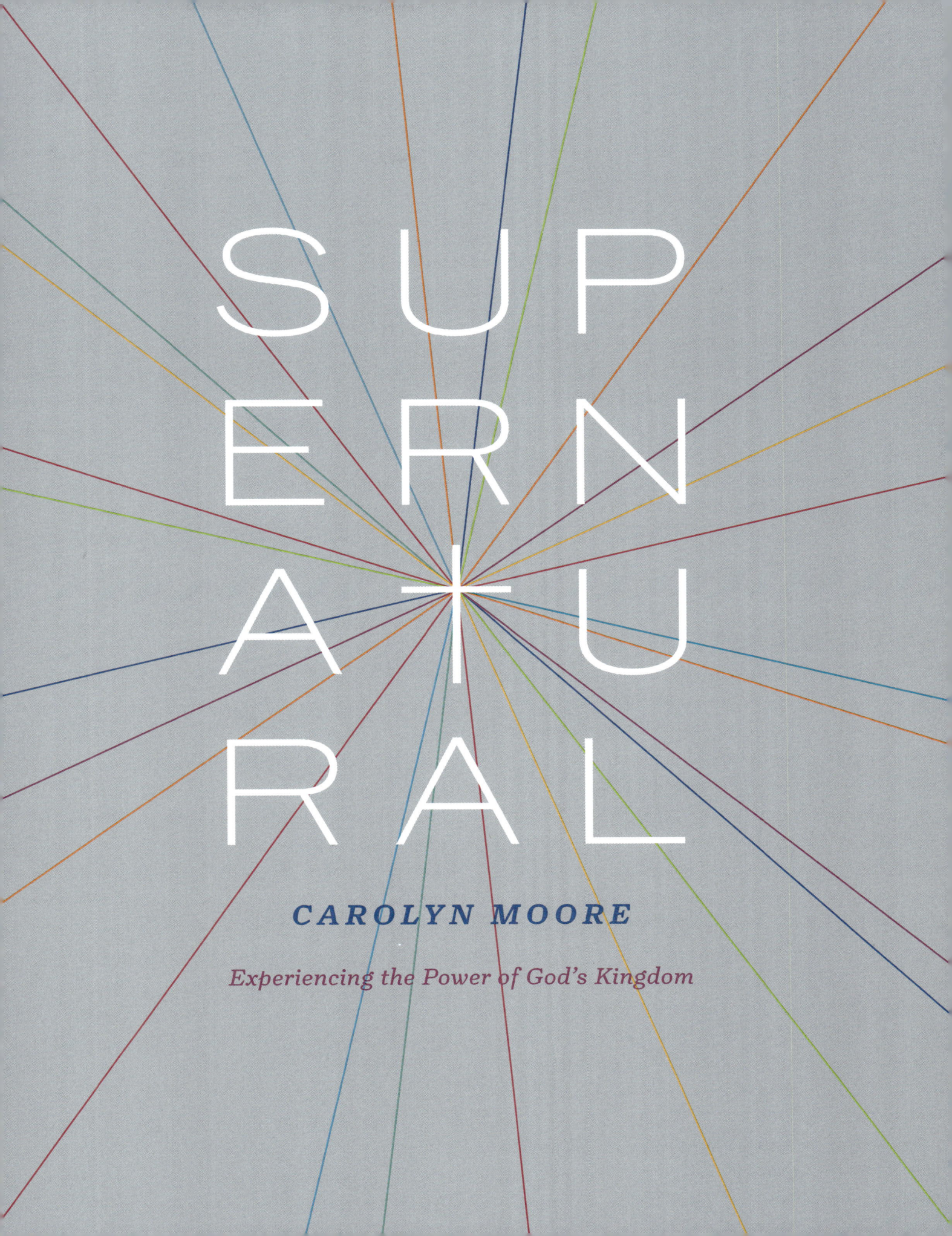

CAROLYN MOORE

Experiencing the Power of God's Kingdom

Copyright 2020 by Carolyn Moore

All rights reserved. No part of this publication may be reproduced, stored in a retrieval system, or transitted, in any form or by any means—electronic, mechanical, photocopying, recording, or otherwise—without prior written permission, except for brief quotations in critical reviews or articles.

Unless otherwise indicated, all Scripture quotations are taken from THE HOLY BIBLE, NEW INTERNATIONAL VERSION®, NIV® copyright © 1973, 1978, 1984, 2011 by Biblica, Inc.® Used by permission. All rights reserved worldwide.

Scripture translations marked ESV are taken from the ESV® Bible (The Holy Bible, English Standard Version®). ESV® Text Edition: 2016. Copyright © 2001 by Crossway, a publishing ministry of Good News Publishers. Used by permission.

Scripture marked MSG are taken from THE MESSAGE, copyright © 1993, 2002, 2018 by Eugene H. Peterson. Used by permission of NavPress. All rights reserved. Represented by Tyndale House Publishers, Inc.

Scripture marked NASB are taken from the NEW AMERICAN STANDARD BIBLE®, copyright © 1960, 1962, 1963, 1968, 1971, 1972, 1973, 1975, 1977, 1995 by The Lockman Foundation. Used by permission.

Scripture marked NLT are taken from the Holy Bible, New Living Translation, copyright © 1996, 2004, 2015 by Tyndale House Foundation. Used by permission of Tyndale House Publishers, Inc., Carol Stream, Illinois 60188. All rights reserved.

Printed in the United States of America

Cover and page design by Strange Last Name

Moore, Carolyn (Pastor)
  Supernatural : experiencing the power of God's kingdom / Carolyn Moore. – Franklin, Tennessee : Seedbed Publishing, ©2020.

  pages ; cm.

  An eight session Bible study with an accompanying teaching video.
  ISBN 9781628247527 (paperback)
  ISBN 9781628247565 (DVD)
  ISBN 9781628247534 (Mobi)
  ISBN 9781628247541 (ePub)
  ISBN 9781628247558 (uPDF)

  1. Power (Christian theology)--Biblical teaching. 2. Holy Spirit. 3. Kingdom of God. 4. Christian life--Methodist authors.
  I. Title.

BT738.25.M66 2020   248.4   2019957578

Seedbed

SEEDBED PUBLISHING
Franklin, Tennessee
Seedbed.com

CONTENTS

How to Use This Book   7

Introduction   9

SECTION ONE

1. Sent People   13
2. The Mark of Supernatural Power   16
3. Just Do It   19
4. Truth Is a Person   22
5. Give What God Gives You   25

Group Gathering: 1–5   28

SECTION TWO

6. Boldly Vulnerable   31
7. The Gospel Is a Miracle   34
8. The Miracle of Chosenness   37
9. What You Believe Matters   40
10. The Gospel of Welcome (Part 1)   43

Group Gathering: 6–10   46

SECTION THREE

11. The Gospel of Welcome (Part 2)   49
12. Let's Eat   52
13. Whom God Pursues   55
14. Gathering a Kingdom Welcome   58
15. What It Means to Be Alive   61

Group Gathering: 11–15   64

SECTION FOUR

16. Surrender and the Supernatural   67
17. I Am the God Who Heals You   70
18. What about Manifestations?   73
19. Awakened   76
20. Check Your Life   79

Group Gathering: 16–20   82

SECTION FIVE

21	From Shame to Grace	85
22	From Shame to Grace . . . to Glory!	88
23	Cloud, Fire, and Glory	91
24	Talking about Glory	94
25	A Religion of Miracles	97

Group Gathering: 21–25 — 100

SECTION SIX

26	What We Know about the Enemy of Our Souls	103
27	Jesus Wins	106
28	The Kingdom Advances	109
29	The Finger of God	112
30	Exposing the Kingdom of God	115

Group Gathering: 26–30 — 118

SECTION SEVEN

31	Shaken, Not Stirred	121
32	But What If I Don't Want To?	124
33	No More Unholy Hesitation!	127
34	Jesus Plans to Wreck Your Life	130
35	But First . . .	133

Group Gathering: 31–35 — 136

SECTION EIGHT

36	Live This	139
37	Being Sent with Living Water	142
38	Do It Again	145
39	Go!	148
40	Receive the Holy Spirit	151

Group Gathering: 36–40 — 154

Notes — 157

HOW TO USE THIS BOOK

Let me warn you now: I have great expectations for you as you begin this study. Through your time in the Word, I expect your understanding of what it means to be a Christian and what it means to be "the church" to be radically changed. I expect, and am praying for you, to become hungry for the infilling of the Holy Spirit, and I earnestly hope you will be bold in seeking out his supernatural power. I am praying that you and I both will come to expect supernatural ministry inside our own communities of faith, and that what we breed in faith will spill out into the world to transform it.

I need to tell you that I am not hoping you will only enjoy this study or that through it you will be able to tweak the practice of your faith. Nope. I'm expecting transformation. Listen, we serve such a glorious God. He is a supernatural force in this world, and he is good. Supernatural results are what I'm expecting through this study because Jesus is supernatural. In other words, I expect you to encounter God—Father, Son, and Holy Spirit—as you open the Word, embrace the wonder, and cry out for more.

There are forty separate entries in this book. You could probably start anywhere and get something out of what you read (though I recommend taking them in order). By simply numbering them, I hope to give you multiple options for using this material. You might choose to use this as a personal devotional study, taking it one at a time over the course of forty days. Or you might gather a group for an eight-week study, reading five each week for eight weeks. Or maybe your group wants to steep in this study over a longer stretch of time, studying one entry each week over most of a year.

Whatever works! That's my advice. As long as you are in this to go deeper into the things of God, I'm your biggest cheerleader. However you read it, be all in. That's what matters.

A teaching video with eight sessions accompanies this study, so you've got that resource to draw from as well. Exercises are structured to give you every opportunity for a deep personal and spiritual experience. A brief section called

HOW TO USE THIS BOOK

"Listening to the Word" at the end of each entry gives you the chance to bring the Word home to live in you. Make the most of those moments. Take the time needed to let God speak.

Rather than providing all the Scripture references within the text, you'll be asked to do the work of finding the passages in your own Bible so you can mark up the sections studied and begin to create a habit of looking for where God is at work in Scripture. Ask the Holy Spirit to help you experience the Bible as the living Word. This is the one book that has the ability to speak a fresh word into your life wherever you are, to be relevant over and over again. That's the power of the living Word.

You'll also want to keep a journal or notebook for this study. Write your responses to the questions in that book. If you will actively participate in this study, you will cultivate devotional practices that will continue long after this guidebook has been shelved.

I often journal in two colors, writing my own thoughts in black or blue ink and what I sense may be Spirit-inspired thoughts in red. When I do this in my own time with God, I don't try to analyze it; I just listen for the voice of the Spirit and write what I hear in red ink. A week or so down the road, I may come back to that entry to see how it sounds with the benefit of a little time and perspective. Often, I am amazed at how helpful those entries can be to my journey with Jesus. I do believe he still speaks into our lives. I have encountered him in the practice of journaling, and I hope you will too.

I hope the combination of this guidebook, your own journal, the creative prayer exercises, and a quiet place to listen to the Word will converge to create a spiritual revival in your life and in your church. Nothing less . . . only *more*.

Know that as you begin, I am praying for you. My friends, I expect great things!

INTRODUCTION

Paul wrote: "I want to know Christ—yes, to know the power of his resurrection. . . . Not that I have already obtained all this, or have already arrived at my goal, but I press on to take hold of that for which Christ Jesus took hold of me" (Phil. 3:10, 12).

I want more.

I am hungry to see the power of the Holy Spirit in our midst.

Hungry.

I'm not talking about so much that passes these days for Spirit-filled experiences. We have defaulted to bragging; we tell too many "big fish stories." We talk of huge moves of God that are not quantified by fruit, and we call our good feelings "moves of the Spirit." My concern is that we sometimes misrepresent the Spirit by assigning to him feats easily accomplished in the natural and by making more of what happens in our corporate gatherings than is actually there.

We have overplayed our hand and become accustomed to calling any emotional response a great move of God. Meanwhile, we are completely shortchanging what must surely be a much more awesome and beautiful power than fleeting experiences that result in no lasting transformation.

What is most disturbing is that we cling to stories of Holy Spirit power in other places at other times, as if by only having heard the stories we can somehow claim participation. While I certainly celebrate with followers of Jesus in other countries who report awesome healings and even resurrections (I believe these to be true), I am not content to let what is happening in other places suffice for my own experience of the person and work of the Holy Spirit.

I am hungry for the power of the Holy Spirit to fall on us . . . *here*. We, too, are responsible not just for learning the lingo and culture of Spirit-filled living but also for watching for the actual work of the Spirit in our churches, our families, and our own lives.

INTRODUCTION

Aren't you hungry for more?

I am starving for it and have decided to lean in and get more intentional about watching for what the Holy Spirit is actually doing right here, right now. I am praying for the kind of personal and corporate renewal that can be attributed to only the power of God. I'm no longer content to be encouraged by a good word or titillated by emotionally charged moments. I want to be changed by the presence and power of the Holy Spirit, and I want that for those I pastor. I want that for you.

In Luke 9–10, the followers of Jesus have power and authority to cast out demons, cure diseases, proclaim the kingdom, and heal the sick. That is a far cry from what we are experiencing in most churches today. Until we are honest about that, I'm not sure we'll be able to move past the weak substitutes for which we've settled. How many of us are willing to stop calling it the power of God when we leave church feeling good about ourselves? How many of us are willing to lean in and start crying out for the real thing?

> I am praying for the kind of personal and corporate renewal that can be attributed to only the power of God. I want to be changed by the presence and power of the Holy Spirit, and I want that for those I pastor. I want that for you.

Don't American Christians also deserve to see the power of God and become conversant in the real and powerful work of the Holy Spirit? Aren't we, their leaders, responsible for properly defining that power and calling our people to that hunger?

The one thing of which I've become most convinced is that for us to have any hope of breaking through to something deeper, we must get honest. Until we stop calling every warm experience a genuine move of God, we won't find the deeper well. It is as if we've found a stagnant pond in the desert and have camped there when an oasis of sweet, pure water is just ahead.

I am hungry for more and tired by less. If you are actually experiencing it, I want to hear your stories—your first-person, real-life, recent, authentic stories of the power of God at work in your own life or in your community. I want to hear first-person healing stories that have resulted in works that glorify God. I want to hear real stories that have resulted in spiritual fruit and advanced the kingdom of God on earth.

I want to hear proof of the authentic, awesome power of God working in our churches, in our lives.

INTRODUCTION

Paul's words resonate deeply with me:

> *I want to know Christ—yes, to know the power of his resurrection and participation in his sufferings, becoming like him in his death, and so, somehow, attaining to the resurrection from the dead. Not that I have already obtained all this, or have already arrived at my goal, but I press on to take hold of that for which Christ Jesus took hold of me. (Phil. 3:10–12)*

I am pressing in and I invite you to join me. I want to know the power that resurrects people from the dead. I want more than just "good church."

Don't you? Yes? Then read on.

SECTION ONE

1

SENT PEOPLE

Key Observation
Unless I miss my guess, most of us in the Western world do not have a wide experience with casting out demons and participating in physical healings.

> **Read Luke 4:18–19, then read Luke 9:1–2.**
> - Mark all the action words in both of these passages, then make a list of those words.
> - What adjectives (descriptive words) do these action words inspire?
> - What new thoughts do you have about the mission of Jesus after reading these two passages together?

As he sat among his people, Jesus cast a vision for a radical change in the spiritual climate. He stood up in the middle of church one day and read from a scroll unrolled to the words of the prophet Isaiah:

*"The Spirit of the Lord is upon me,
because he has anointed me
to proclaim good news to the poor.
He has sent me to proclaim freedom for the prisoners
and recovery of sight for the blind,
to set the oppressed free,
to proclaim the year of the Lord's favor." (Luke 4:18–19)*

What a bold proclamation! Jesus, standing on the authority of the Spirit, was staking his claim as the first apostle and prototype of this good news. Yes, Jesus was and is an apostle! Had you considered that fact before? The term in Greek literally means "sent one." In that sense, Jesus most definitely fit the definition. He was sent to earth by the will of God the Father with very specific

SUPERNATURAL

marching orders—to reveal the kingdom to the poor, the prisoners, the blind, the oppressed, and those who have never felt favor with God. He was sent to cast out demons, cure diseases, proclaim the kingdom, and heal the sick. In Luke 4, he does this. He drives out multiple demons, heals quite a few people, and calls down favor over a tax collector, a few fishermen, and some other misfits who are invited into his inner circle to watch and learn what it means to be sent ones.

> We are not shooting for tolerable. We are shooting for transformation and for lives that carry power and authority.

That's Luke chapter 4. From there until chapter 9, it is wall-to-wall ministry. Then in Luke 9, there is a shift: Jesus recast the vision, but this time he did so by sharing power with his followers. He pulled the twelve disciples together, and "he gave them power and authority to drive out all demons and to cure diseases, and he sent them out to proclaim the kingdom of God and to heal the sick" (Luke 9:1–2). Can you imagine? This was a high calling for this gaggle of misfits.

- Can you even imagine what that charge must have felt like for those first followers of Jesus?
- How would you receive such a charge?
- Have you ever had the experience of God calling you to a task you felt utterly unequipped to accomplish?

Jesus' followers were told they now had both the authority and power to do what they'd seen only one other person do, and what they saw was so remarkable that they assigned divinity to the man doing it. It must have been stunning. Those regular, not-the-brightest-bulb-in-the-box people were sent out to drive out demons and cure diseases and proclaim the kingdom and heal the sick. They would become the culture changers! They would welcome and advance the kingdom of God by bearing fruit in their "sent-ness." This was the first work of the Twelve, whom we call apostles—the "sent-out ones."

There is a catch, of course, to this kind of sending. To drive out demons, you have to get within spitting distance of demon-possessed people (many of whom spit!). To heal, you have to touch people with all manner of disease. To proclaim the kingdom, you have to associate with heathens. You must get up close and personal with the poor, the prisoners, the blind, and the oppressed. That was and is the offer on the table because that, Jesus said, is how climates change and the kingdom comes.

Now, hold that paradigm up against what many of us experience in the American church today. Unless I miss my guess, most of us in the Western

SENT PEOPLE

world do not have a wide experience with casting out demons and participating in physical healings. It happens in developing countries where first generation Christians don't know any better—that is a bit of missional humor; of course, our friends in other countries certainly "know better." In many other countries, Christians are running circles around us in spiritual revival right now.

Our culture has come to accept an hour in church and a blessing before meals as the center of the Christian experience. Meanwhile, driving out demons is just weird. We relegate that to the fringe. But folks, this is how Jesus defined for his followers what it means to be sent out to represent the very best the kingdom has to offer this world: that followers have power and authority to drive out demons, cure diseases, proclaim the kingdom of God, and heal things that destroy people's lives.

This ought to be our target as we progress in the Christian life. We are not shooting for tolerable. We are shooting for transformation and for lives that carry power and authority. Let that sink in.

LISTENING TO THE WORD

As we begin this study together, write a prayer in your journal, expressing your own honest feelings about God's power, your part in his plan, your doubts, your hopes. Pray, asking God to fill you with his Holy Spirit and for him to give you ears to hear what the Spirit is saying to you throughout this study.

2

THE MARK OF SUPERNATURAL POWER

Key Observation.
To be incarnational means to embody the Spirit of Christ.

Read Luke 9:1–2
- List all the things Jesus does for his followers in those two verses.
- Now list all the things he empowers them to do.
- How did the twelve disciples get their power and authority?
- How do you suppose they knew when it was given to them?

Yep, I know we've already read the first two verses of Luke 9. We're reading them again today and will continue reading them throughout this study because I believe they represent Jesus' deep hopes for people who are sent out in his name. Why do I believe that? Well, because these are the words he used when he sent folks out in his name. He sent them out with power and authority to cast out demons, cure diseases, proclaim the kingdom, and heal the sick.

A friend in our community often argues with me (in a good way) about the mark of the Holy Spirit in a life. I say the mark of the Holy Spirit is a supernatural ability to love, basing my thoughts on Paul's teaching. He wrote, "The fruit of the Spirit is love, joy, peace, forbearance, kindness, goodness, faithfulness, gentleness and self-control" (Gal. 5:22–23). All these flow from the

THE MARK OF SUPERNATURAL POWER

Spirit, and you'll notice that in that list love is the headwaters. Our ability to love is not self-generated or self-taught. It comes to us directly from the Holy Spirit.

The mark of the Holy Spirit is a supernatural ability to love, right?

My friend argues the mark of the Holy Spirit is power, and he looks to Acts 1:8 to make his point, where Jesus said, "You will receive power when the Holy Spirit comes on you; and you will be my witnesses in Jerusalem, and in all Judea and Samaria, and to the ends of the earth." Clearly, Jesus wanted his followers to know that power to evangelize would come with the call to go. "You *will* receive power," Jesus said. Not "you *might* receive" or "if you're lucky you'll receive." Nope. Jesus said, "You *will* receive power."

So, which is it? Love or power? The answer—wait for it—is yes. I suspect (though I'd really rather be right) that we're both right and that in kingdom terms, *love* and *power* are two ways of talking about the same thing. In the kingdom of God, love is power, and power is always loving. Power is never self-serving, and love is never wimpy (you should underline that). When Jesus gave his followers power, it was the kind that drove them out to heal, along with a heart broken for those who hurt. Love drove them out to meet people exactly where they were, with power strong enough to call out demons and overcome disease. In other words, they were not sent out with raw power and no heart. They were sent out as Christ-bearers, to be and do incarnational ministry in both the love and power of Christ.

> Our call is to receive the power and authority offered us by Christ himself, then to go forth as he sends us to drive out the darkness and expose the kingdom of God.

To be incarnational means to embody the spirit of Christ. It means we don't go on our own power and authority, but on his. And that brings up a critical point made in today's passage: *kingdom power and kingdom authority are gifts from God.* We don't generate them on our own steam. Our power and authority to carry out supernatural ministry are gifts, an anointing of the Holy Spirit. And this is why we must pursue the infilling of the Holy Spirit. Without him, we are sunk.

Don't attempt supernatural ministry on your own strength. Because you can actually *do* ministry without the Holy Spirit. People do all kinds of good things without supernatural power. All day, every day, people operate out of their own talents on their own authority. Take the word of a recovering striver. Plenty of us are driven by ambition or fear or even a good heart and good intentions to do good things (I am literally sitting across the table right now from an atheist I've befriended who works at a food bank). And when they do, they achieve *natural* results, not *supernatural* results.

But, folks, this is not the biblical call. Our call is to receive the power and authority offered us by Christ himself, then to go forth as he sends us to drive out the darkness and expose the kingdom of God. If we're going to give the world a better definition of "church," we need the infilling and empowerment of the Holy Spirit, so we can actually witness *supernatural* ministry.

> ### Read Luke 11:2–4
> - Compare this prayer that Jesus taught his followers with the charge he gave them in Luke 9:1–2. Taking this prayer and this charge together, what do you learn about the values of Jesus?
> - What matters to him?
> - What miracles are Jesus calling for in his prayer?

In Luke 9, Jesus imparted kingdom power and kingdom authority to a few people who had been following him, and he charged them to go out and become the answer to his own prayer. And that is still our charge today. It is to become the answer to Jesus' prayer. We are sent people, because Jesus, who was sent by God, is still with us. He is still at work in our world welcoming and advancing the kingdom of God, and he will not stop until the kingdom comes and God's will is fully realized on earth as it is in heaven.

LISTENING TO THE WORD

Let's get honest here. Where in your life do you need to humbly admit that your ministry or work is more about natural effort and good intention and less about the power of God? Where have you become tired of the striving? Where are you settling for tolerable when God wants to create transformation? List those places in your journal, then pray that God will make you hungry for more.

3

JUST DO IT

Key Observation:
If we do our part and pray, he'll do his part and show up.

Read Luke 9:1–2
- When Jesus sent out his twelve disciples, what charge did he give them?
- How do you suppose they responded when Jesus laid this spiritual expectation and invitation on them?

Years ago, I had the experience of seeing a demon leave a man's body. He came to my office to complain, and that day he was in a seriously contrary mood. He complained about everything, and as he went on and on, for about an hour, his complaints became more and more personal. Eventually, I'd had enough. It might not have been my best pastoral moment, but I got angry. I began to *discuss*, let's say, with some vigor how I felt about his attack. Almost immediately as I began to speak, however, I had the sense that the person to whom I was talking was not this man in front of me but some demonic force. I can't tell you why I thought it was inside his chest, but in the moment that's where my energies were focused. My eyes were drawn to his chest, and I began to speak directly to the demon. (I am not saying this is how it ought to be when we pray for people or against demonic forces. I'm just telling you how it was for me that day.) The experience became pretty intense rather quickly. I'm sure I was louder than I meant to be. I was clinging to some authority that rose up within me, and I was not about to let that thing, whatever it was, get the upper hand.

I kept speaking intensely to it until it was gone. For a moment after I went silent, the guy, who never moved or said a word while I was casting this demon out, stared at me. Then he sank down in the chair almost as if he were lifeless.

SUPERNATURAL

He didn't fall out of the chair, but I could see that all the energy it took to hold himself up was gone.

We stayed silent for a few beats, then the man looked at me and said, "It's gone. I feel absolutely no anger. In fact, I can't *make* myself get angry with you right now. It's gone." We prayed again, and he left my office. He later told me he could hardly make it to his car before he collapsed in exhaustion. He stayed in the parking lot for half an hour, then drove home and slept for the rest of the day.

Lest you assume I was indoctrinated into this practice early in life, think again. I am probably more like you than not. I grew up in a mainline Protestant church. I could hardly *explain* the Holy Spirit, much less *experience* him. When I entered seminary in my thirties, let's just say I was not the brightest bulb in the seminary box. And yet, God has filled me and schooled me in the Holy Spirit, and I believe this is what he wants for all of us. I believe Jesus longs to see his church acting as if he is a supernatural God and supernatural power is ours.

- What questions do you have about demons or demonic activity?
- What concerns are raised in your spirit as this topic is discussed?
- Can you take those concerns and pray about them?

I believe that Jesus has given us power and authority over not only demons but also physical and emotional illness. Recently, I witnessed a miracle. A woman who was blind in one eye (the result of a stroke six months prior) had been told by a doctor that the loss of her eyesight was permanent. He likened it to a lightning bolt shooting through her eye.

> **I believe Jesus longs to see his church acting as if he is a supernatural God and supernatural power is ours.**

That's the woman I met—blind in one eye, unable to drive any more, and resolved to live with it. Then the Holy Spirit showed up. At the retreat, she was given the gift of profound inner healing. She experienced a touch that left her feeling worthy and loved. She went home and told her husband she'd never felt so free. The next morning, after a strangely peaceful sleep, she awoke to find she could see her husband. He was laying on the side nearest her blind eye, so that was kind of a deal. Her blind eye wasn't blind any more. For the next two hours, they tested her eye in every way they could think of to make sure this was real. It was.

What if this woman's inner healing opened the way for her physical healing? What if it is all much more connected than we realize? And if so, how do we detect the difference between spiritual and physical illnesses? How do we know

JUST DO IT

when and how God is going to move? After decades of praying with people in faith and watching the results, here is my best, most spiritual answer to your question: I don't know.

Seriously . . . *I don't know*.

But in the absence of knowing, I subscribe to Nike's school of thought on this: *Just do it*. Just pray for people. Pray for them like Jesus is listening and like Jesus wants to see healing at least as much as you do. And on the days when you don't believe it will ever happen, pray in obedience as Scripture commands (see James 5). I figure, if we do our part and pray, he'll do his part and show up.

And here's the thing: If you're wrong, *nobody dies*.[1] If you pray and nothing happens, at least you prayed. At least you called on some force greater than yourself, and you practiced faith in the process. Those are good things, their own kind of miracle, because hope in a supernatural God is a rare and glorious thing.

LISTENING TO THE WORD

End this session by asking God to show you how to get ready to receive his power and authority to cast out demons, cure diseases, proclaim the kingdom, and heal the sick. Ask him to reveal what you need to abandon so you can be "all in" for this charge. And then ask for courage to move when he moves.

4

TRUTH IS A PERSON

Key Observation
"Aim at Heaven, and you will get earth 'thrown in': aim at earth, and you will get neither." —C. S. Lewis

Read Luke 9:1–2.
- We've now read these lines through multiple times. Can you close your Bible and say them from memory?
- What are the key phrases from these two verses? What is the priority?
- How do you hear Jesus' voice when you imagine him giving these instructions to his followers? Is he enthusiastic? Serious? Passionate? Concerned?
- What word would you use to describe him? What word would you use to describe the Twelve as they listen to Jesus?

The only power worth pursuing is power borrowed from faith in the gospel of Jesus Christ. Life is too short, your time too limited, and your skills too valuable to be spent on anything less than kingdom work accomplished in kingdom power. I'm thinking about that famous quote from C. S. Lewis: "Aim at Heaven and you will get earth 'thrown in': aim at earth and you will get neither."[2] Addressing the physical needs and emotional discomforts of people without offering them the good news of Jesus Christ is like aiming for earth instead of heaven. In other words, we have a *Person*-centered faith, not a *people*-centered faith. We love people, and we are passionate about the things that break God's heart. But to have anything of value to offer people, we have to go through the heart of God to the Person of Jesus. Otherwise, we'll land short of the kingdom.

TRUTH IS A PERSON

This is exactly what Jesus warned his followers at the end of Luke 9. He essentially said, "You will have a thousand excuses for why you can't do this. You'll be glad to do good things on your own steam, but you will not want the cost of proclaiming the kingdom. And, friend, while that may provide temporary relief, it will be devastating in the long run. To get to life—*real* life—you will have to carry the whole gospel."

> **Read Luke 9:57–62.**
> - Read verse 60 again. What do you think Jesus meant by his response?
> - Is there more than one possible meaning at work here?

In my Bible, I've written the word *paralysis* in big red letters above these verses. Luke, who gave us example after example of people who got right up to the line of surrender, froze. It's as if the idea of going with Jesus was more appealing than the reality. It reminds me of the scene where Moses talked to God face-to-face (Ex. 33:12–23). God tested him at just this point, saying, effectively, "I'm not going with you, because you are a stubborn bunch" (my paraphrase of Exodus 33:3). Moses got alone with God, shared intimately in his presence, and then responded with one of the most profound questions in the Old Testament, maybe the whole Bible. He asked, "If your Presence does not go with us . . . how will anyone know that you are pleased with me and with your people . . . ? What else will distinguish me and your people from all the other people on the face of the earth?" (vv. 15–16).

It's a profound question. What exactly makes us—the church—any different from any other well-run nonprofit, or even the nonprofits that aren't run so well? If God isn't in it and if we aren't intimately aware of his presence among us, what makes us any different? Brothers and sisters in Christ, I have late-breaking news for you. You're not in church to learn how to run a nonprofit. You've been called to step into a great move of the Holy Spirit, a move that will often take you way outside your comfort zone.

> **No waffling, no shirking back, no getting ahead of God. Either go with Jesus, or don't go at all.**

"How will anyone know that you are pleased with me and with your people unless you go with us?" There's to be no waffling, no shirking back, no getting ahead of God. Either go with Jesus, or don't go at all.

This is the essence of the charge in Luke 9:1–2. It is Jesus who sent his followers out with his power and authority—the power and authority from his own stash that he laid on them. It is Jesus, who sent them out with *his* truth. *Proclaim the kingdom*, he told them. To proclaim the kingdom is to proclaim Jesus. So it turns out that truth is not a set of facts; truth is a person.

Do you know that truth? Do you have a personal experience of him? If someone showed up at your table in Starbucks and asked you the reason for your hope, what would you tell them? Think it'll never happen? Did I mention that I'm sitting at Starbucks right now, across the table from my atheist friend? If you don't already have a simple way to share the gospel with someone, try reading these sermons from some of the first followers of Jesus:

✶ Peter's sermon in Acts 2:14–40
✶ Stephen's sermon in Acts 7:1–53
✶ Paul's sermon in Acts 13:17–39

How grateful I am for the faith of powerfully courageous men and women who laid down their lives for the sake of this precious, life-giving, miracle-working good news. What a privilege it is to stand on their shoulders and find our place in that great cloud of witnesses!

LISTENING TO THE WORD

Is your heart full of a desire to do good things for people, or is your heart full of Jesus? Because your mouth will speak what your heart is full of. The beauty of the gospel is that when rightly ordered, one will lead to the other. A heart full of Jesus will lead to a desire to do good things for people! So, are you deeply, passionately, all-out in love with Jesus? If you cannot honestly say right now that you are in love with Jesus, then please stop everything and cry out to God, asking him to restore (or give) you a fresh passion for him. Ask for it. Flat-out ask. Don't wait. Don't hedge. Jesus wants your heart, so this is a prayer he is likely to answer.

5

GIVE WHAT GOD GIVES YOU

Key Observation
This invitation to participate with the Holy Spirit in the works he wants to do in the world is an invitation into partnership.

Read Luke 9:1–6 and then read Matthew 10:1–15.
- On a sheet of paper or in your journal, make two columns with these two headings: "Similarities" and "Differences." Now, comb through these passages and make a note under "Similarities" of everything that seems similar in the two passages. Then under "Differences" make notes of anything you find in one passage that you don't find in the other.
- If you had to boil down all of Jesus' instructions in these two passages to a simple one-sentence commission to the disciples, what would it be?

When I read the details of Jesus' commissioning of these missionaries, I have fresh respect for those first followers. Clearly, Jesus wanted to strip them of any sense of self-sufficiency so he could create in them a holy dependence on him.

It is curious that Jesus doesn't want them to take anything with them. After all, these are the descendants of those first Israelites who walked out of Egypt with Egyptian silver and gold clanking under their cloaks. Taking with them everything the Egyptians handed over was a sign that God was with them. That silver and gold was poured back into the tabernacle that housed the presence of God. Yet now as they are sent out again with the promises of God, they are told to take nothing. So, when it comes to being sent, on which principle should we rely? Should we take stuff? Or no stuff?

Here's what I suspect. I suspect the answer is yes.

SUPERNATURAL

If God gives you resources to build the kingdom, use them. If he gives you a great building, a lot of culturally relevant bling, and every convenience at your fingertips, use it. But if he doesn't, go anyway. Because at the end of the day, it isn't the stuff God uses. It is the cloud and the fire that made the tent into the tabernacle, and it is the Holy Spirit that gives an apostle power and authority. The stuff is useful but not necessary. Most miracles happen for free.

The spiritual principle is this: give what God gives you. Write that on a Post-it note and put it on your bathroom mirror. I want this statement to condition you every day to go out and pour out what God pours in. Lay hands on people. Pray. Call down the power of God. That costs nothing except a little pride, and you probably have a little of that to spare.

> **You are called to go and take with you whatever you are given, with the absolute confidence that God will use it to advance his kingdom on earth.**

There is another scene in the book of Acts where the disciples of Jesus are out doing good things without any physical resources. Because the scene happens after the resurrection and ascension of Jesus, we know Peter and John have taken to heart what Jesus taught them while he was with them.

Read Acts 3:1–10.
- What image comes to mind when you first meet the man in this passage?
- Why do you suppose he calls out specifically to Peter and John? Do you think they are among many whom he is asking for alms, or is there something particular about them that grabs his attention?
- Why do you suppose Peter responds as he does, saying, "Look at us!" (v. 4)? What is gained by asking the man to look at Peter?

By the power of the Holy Spirit, Peter sees the man healed in a moment. Write down all the reasons you can think of why God might have accomplished a miracle in this man's life. Why this man? Why this place? Why through Peter and John?

In this scene, we see the teaching of Jesus come full circle. In Luke 9, he sent out the Twelve to heal, save, and deliver. He told them to take nothing with them. When they went, they could not completely understand the "why" behind Jesus' instructions, but by the time they had returned from that first missionary journey, they were convinced. They had seen the power of God overshadow any physical comforts they may have had or shared.

GIVE WHAT GOD GIVES YOU

Now that Jesus had ascended and the apostles were serving on their own, they had owned Jesus' teaching. That was how they rolled. They had learned to offer nothing but the power of God. They understood themselves as walking vessels of the kingdom, and they appreciated the treasure of that. I can tell you that in our ministry at Mosaic (the church I pastor), this has been a huge lesson for us. We have discovered that the quickest way to squelch the work of the Holy Spirit in a relationship is to throw money at a need. That unbalances the power dynamic in a bad way. Yes, sometimes funds and stuff are exactly what's needed, but much more often the relationship is the real treasure.

When the Holy Spirit invites us to participate in the works he wants to do in the world, it is an invitation into a partnership. It changes how we approach life. It is about becoming open to the opportunities around us. If you have accepted the Holy Spirit into your life, you are a tabernacle—a sent-out person with kingdom power to see miracles happen. This is who you are. You are called to go and take with you whatever you are given, with the absolute confidence that God will use it to advance his kingdom on earth.

LISTENING TO THE WORD

Give what God gives you. So what has God given you? Make a personal inventory of every asset in your life. List everything—personality traits, house, car, funds, talents, connections, spiritual gifts, experiences . . . all of it. Now, place it before God and ask him how he plans to use all you've got to welcome and advance his kingdom.

Group Gathering

OPEN WITH PRAYER

WATCH SESSION 1 VIDEO

DISCUSS THE FOLLOWING QUESTIONS BASED ON READINGS 1–5

1

Key Observation
Unless I miss my guess, most of us in the Western world do not have wide experience with casting out demons and participating in physical healings.

Question for Discussion
As you begin this study, how comfortable are you with the idea that following Jesus includes casting out demons, curing disease, proclaiming the kingdom, and healing the sick?

2

Key Observation
To be incarnational means to embody the Spirit of Christ.

Question for Discussion
How does the word "incarnational" help you to think about the power and purpose of supernatural ministry?

3

Key Observation
If we do our part and pray, he'll do his part and show up.

Question for Discussion
What if it is all much more connected than we realize? Does this thought inspire possible connections in your own life between seemingly unrelated wounds and ailments?

4

Key Observation
"Aim at Heaven, and you will get earth 'thrown in': aim at earth, and you will get neither." —C. S. Lewis

Question for Discussion
How has the church (not your church specifically, but the broader church) missed its aim for heaven, and how has this impacted our effectiveness as Christians?

5

Key Observation
This invitation to participate with the Holy Spirit in the works he wants to do in the world is an invitation into partnership.

Question for Discussion
How would it change your approach to prayer and ministry if you began to think of yourself in partnership with Jesus for the sake of exposing the kingdom of God on earth?

CLOSE WITH PRAYER

This study is an invitation to interact with a group *inside* the Holy Spirit. Think of this group as a crucible or petri dish, and your conversations as an experiment in growing supernatural faith. Begin the experiment here by spending time in listening prayer. Each of you should listen quietly, pen in hand, and write down anything you hear. Trust the Holy Spirit to speak. Have someone close in prayer, then share any key ideas for the edification of the group.

SECTION TWO

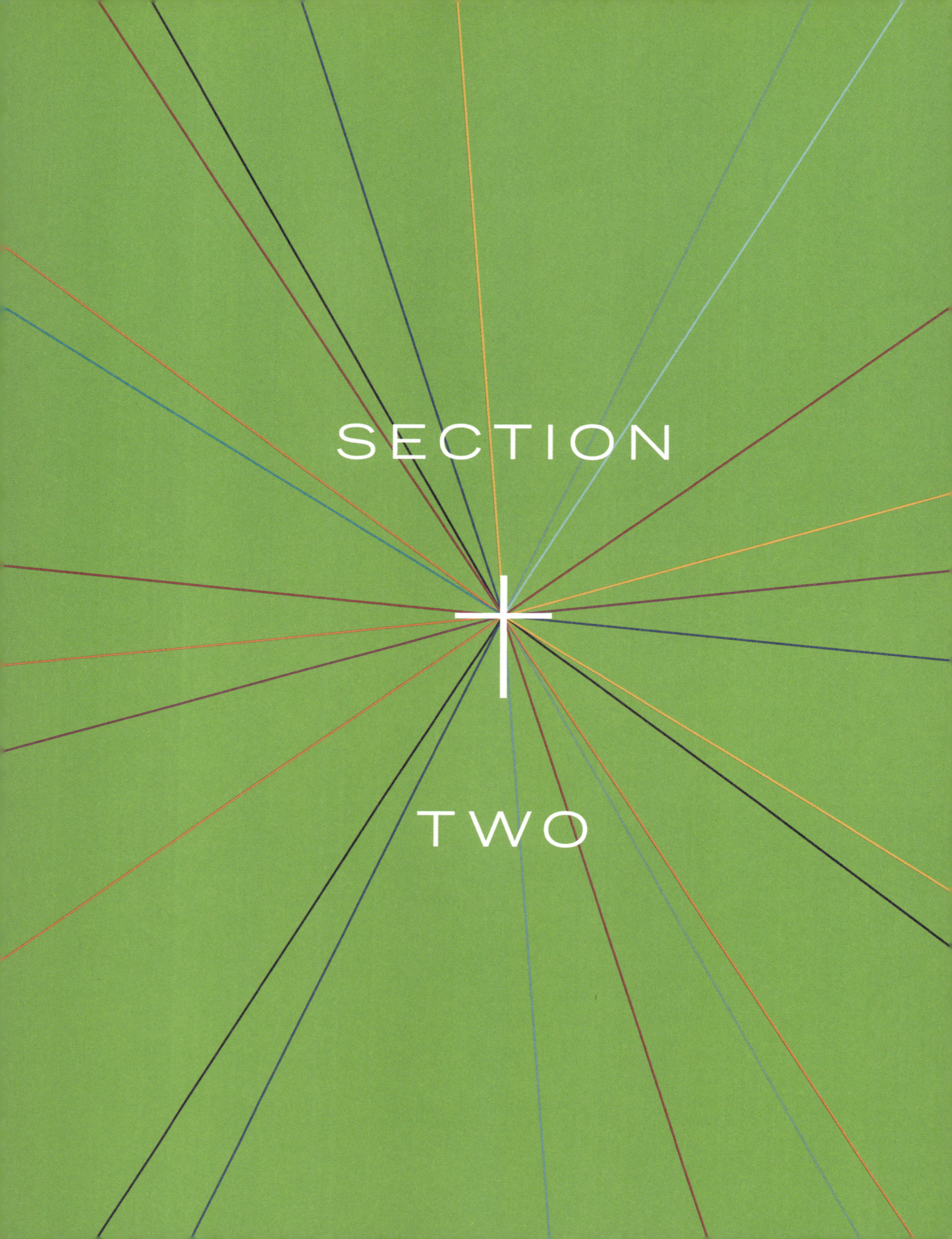

6

BOLDLY VULNERABLE

Key Observation
It is a risky thing, but healthy, to step out into that mixture of doubt and faith, trusting like crazy he will show up and lead you through.

Read Luke 7:18–23 and Matthew 11:2–6.
- How might John have heard from prison about the work of Jesus?
- What does John's question tell you about his values? What is important to John?

Compare Matthew 11:4–5 with what you read in Luke 9:1–2 and also Luke 4:18–19.
- What do you learn about Jesus from this comparison?
- What is important to Jesus? According to these verses, what are his values?

In Luke 9, Herod asks one very important question that ties together several key scenes: Who is Jesus? That is surely the most important question any of us will ever answer for ourselves. Until that question is settled in some deep place within us, nothing else matters. And once we get that answer right, everything else makes sense. Let's follow the thread of that question through several scenes in the stories of John, Jesus, and Herod.

First, a word about Herod. He is referred to in the Bible as Herod the Tetrarch, Herod Antipas, or King Herod. When you see those names in the story of Jesus, keep in mind that they are all the same guy. Herod was a minor political figure who wreaked havoc on the early Christian movement. He ruthlessly killed John the Baptist after imprisoning him. He participated in the condemnation and murder of Jesus himself. He killed James (the brother of John). He persecuted the early church. In other words, this was one mean dude. I'm pretty sure he had anger issues and was probably not voted "most altruistic" for his school yearbook.

Herod's life intersected with John's when John began prophesying about the coming of a rival king and performing miracles that got the attention of the masses. This threatened Herod. If we're honest, this same thing threatens some of us today. David Watson, professor of theology at United Seminary, wrote:

> *Most Christians are entirely comfortable talking about gifts of wisdom and faith. But healing? Miraculous powers? Prophecy? These may be harder to believe— but why? Simply put, the less a particular gift seems to require of God, the easier it is for us to believe. We have been taught not to expect very much of God, and our prayers match those expectations. We may or may not actively disbelieve in these gifts, but passive disbelief in them is quite common.*[3]

The further "out there" a person gets with the power of Jesus, the more of a threat she or he becomes to the rest of us who aren't there yet. Herod is the poster child for that. He had John tossed into prison just for being John, and now John wanted to make sure this was worth it. Of Jesus, he asked, "Is this guy the one?" (see Matthew 11:3). As C. S. Lewis famously framed it, either he is and is worth dying for or he is a lunatic, in which case John and his followers need to keep looking.[4] Since John needed to know, he sent a few of his students to Jesus to ask, "Are you the one?" Jesus' answer is full of grace and truth: "You tell John this. The blind see, the lame walk, people are hearing good news about the kingdom of God for a change. It is downright scandalous, but may God bless the ones who are not offended by it" (see Matt. 11:4–6, author's paraphrase).

> **To the extent that we don't really understand Jesus and are uncomfortable with the cosmic-kingdom side of him, we will also wrestle with our own identity as his followers.**

I love Jesus for that response. There he is, standing in the middle of a marketplace healing people and talking to people and loving people and the whole time, he understands that healing and preaching and doing the work of the kingdom is probably offending more people than it is attracting. The choice to carry the power of God into the world, even when it means carrying the potential for offense, is a choice to be boldly vulnerable. And that, above all else, describes the heart of Jesus.

BOLDLY VULNERABLE

Speaking of Jesus, Herod asked, "Who is this about whom I hear such things?" (Luke 9:9 ESV).

This Jesus is humbly courageous. He suffered every possible misunderstanding, arrogance, and ignorance yet continues to love radically. This Jesus offended legalists and people bound by a spirit of religion, and he kept healing people anyway, even on days reserved for worshiping the holy God, because maybe healing is worship too. This Jesus laid hands on lepers and dead people and women with demons, imparting the gift of resurrection to them. How offensive that is to those who miss the humanity in bruised souls and snuffed-out spirits!

Jesus was *boldly* vulnerable.

What Jesus did—and what Herod asked—challenges the hidden prejudices in us. To the extent that we don't really understand Jesus and are uncomfortable with the cosmic-kingdom side of him, we will also wrestle with our own identity as his followers. We may secretly take offense ourselves when others claim supernatural ministry because it exposes our own passivity.

If that is you, then here's my advice: deal with it. Seriously. Let Jesus in on your wrestling. Even if it feels uncomfortable, I encourage you to trust a good God with those offenses and defenses and fears and prejudices and even your quiet doubts. It is a risky thing, but it is healthy to step out into that mixture of doubt and faith, trusting like crazy that he will show up and lead you through. Admit to him the parts you struggle to understand because *Jesus* gets it. He gets our fears. He gets the danger of supernatural ministry.

Who is this Jesus about whom we hear such things? This Jesus is full of grace and truth. And this Jesus isn't out to make us comfortable. Nah. He wants to make us great.

LISTENING TO THE WORD

> What offenses, doubts, and fears do you bring to the conversation about Jesus and his supernatural power to heal, save, and deliver? Spend time now in confession, exploring your questions and doubts. Then end with a prayer that God might fill you with a fresh dose of faith in his power to heal, save, and deliver.

7

THE GOSPEL IS A MIRACLE

Key Observation
What Jesus wants from every person who follows him is a clear witness.

Read Luke 9:18–20.
- How do you envision Jesus in prayer? How do you envision his friends praying together with him?
- Jesus asked them, "Who do the crowds say that I am?" (v. 18 ESV). Who are "the crowds"?
- Describe how you suspect Peter must have experienced the moment when Jesus spoke directly to him about his confession of faith. Was he proud, honored, happy, fearful, or humbled?

The father of a dear friend traveled a lot by car, and once when he was out in some rural area in North Carolina, he got turned around. So he stopped and asked a man, "I'm trying to get to Charlotte. Does it make a difference up here at this intersection if I go right or left?" The man replied, "Not to me, it don't."

We would like to think it doesn't really matter whether we go right or left, as long as we get to heaven. We want to believe it doesn't really matter how we live now, as long as we say we believe in Jesus. Or at least in a generic God.

Ah, but nothing in the life of Christ or the witness of his first followers attests to that notion! Jesus wants every person who follows him to give a clear witness: "You are the Christ, God's Messiah, and I will stand for you and die for you, Jesus." Can you say that like you mean it?

THE GOSPEL IS A MIRACLE

When Jesus sent his followers out (Luke 9:1–2), he placed proclaiming the kingdom in the same list as casting out demons, curing diseases, and healing the sick. He clearly considered a decision to accept the good news about Jesus just as miraculous and exciting as any physical miracle. In fact, there are other stories in the Bible of people professing faith, and those stories are clearly told as if a miracle had happened. Do you remember Zacchaeus, the wee little man? We sang his song when we were kids. Zacchaeus climbed up a tree as a seeker and came down as a follower. His encounter with Jesus changed his life. In the course of a dinner party, a swindler became a holy man. Talk about a miracle!

> **Read Luke 19:1–10.**
> - What do you notice about Zacchaeus? What is he like? What gets noticed by the writer?
> - According to this story, what does Jesus value?
> - Read verse 9 again. Jesus makes a proclamation of salvation here. What do you notice about Jesus' statement?
> - What does verse 10 teach (or remind) you about the mission of Jesus?

There is a really cool factor in this story. The pattern of it—language and structure—is the same as other healing stories told in Luke. I'm guessing that is not a coincidence. I have to believe Jesus considered salvation to be just as much of a miracle worth celebrating as any other supernatural act he performed. In fact, I would go so far as to say that the point of all the other miracles is to get people in the same boat with Zacchaeus. Miracles prime the pump for the main message—the truth of the risen Christ who has come to redeem the world.

I have a friend in India who has adopted a few dozen children (yes, you read that right, a few dozen; no, she does not live in a shoe). Some of them came to her through the work of an Indian social worker who'd rescued many kids living on the streets over the years.

This social worker sounds like a kingdom treasure. She once traveled into a rural area to serve a tribal community. When she got there, the people of the village made sure she knew not to go near a certain tree that stood in the center of their village. This tree was cursed, they said. People had died under it. Stay clear of it, especially after dark.

The social worker knew this tree didn't have any such power but no amount of talking could convince the people otherwise. Since she couldn't convince them, she decided to show them. At the end of her day, after doing her job with them, she laid out her bed under that tree and announced she'd be sleeping there.

The village leaders were mortified. They begged her not to do it. They didn't want her blood on their hands.

She refused to listen.

That night, the social worker slept peacefully under that tree, and the next morning she woke up to find herself surrounded by a great cloud of witnesses. The entire village was watching anxiously to see if she'd live to see the sunrise. They'd even invited some folks from a neighboring village. Seeing the crowd, she stood up beneath that tree and shared the great news about Jesus Christ and the power of God Almighty. In one day, most who lived in that village became followers of Jesus.

> The gospel is its own power. It doesn't tell us how to *get* power. It *is* power.

Tell me the proclamation of the kingdom is not a miracle!

My friends, the gospel is its own power. It doesn't tell us how to get power. It is power. Paul told the Romans, "I am not ashamed of this Good News about Christ. It is the power of God at work, saving everyone who believes" (1:16 NLT). Hallelujah.

LISTENING TO THE WORD

Do you remember when you first believed? Have you written that story down? If you haven't yet written your story, now would be a good time. Write it in three simple paragraphs: 1) who you were before you came to believe in Jesus; 2) what happened to cause you to change; and 3) who you are now. That story is proof that you have seen a miracle: your own.

8

THE MIRACLE OF CHOSENNESS

Key Observation
In thinking about Peter's transformation from average disciple to eloquent apostle, we are invited to imagine the personal transformation that had to occur for Peter to stand confidently in this moment and profess this kind of faith.

> ### Read Luke 9:18–20 again, then compare it with the same story in Matthew 16:13–20.
> - What is similar? What is different?
> - What do you learn about Peter from Matthew 16:16–17?
> - What do you learn about Jesus? About the kingdom? About the church?
> - What reasons might Jesus have had for asking them to keep this moment private? What does this request teach you about how the kingdom of God works?

Imagine the personal transformation that had to occur for Peter to stand confidently in this moment and profess this kind of faith. This isn't like changing your opinion on which flavor of ice cream is your favorite. Peter's entire worldview had to be deconstructed. His understanding of the Jewish Messiah had to be rebuilt based on the reality of who Jesus was. Literally, Peter had to be reborn, with a whole new mind-set.

To be honest, Peter reminds me of . . . *us*. He is a regular guy, not voted most likely to be talked about two thousand years later. Yet this is the guy who first publicly professed Jesus as God. This is the guy Jesus tapped to send his message forward. You have to admire the man. He may have stumbled along the way, but he definitely figured out how to fall forward.

SUPERNATURAL

The Message version of this scene in Matthew between Jesus and Peter is a beautiful picture of Jesus seeing in Peter what he may not yet have see in himself:

He pressed them, "And how about you? Who do you say I am?"

Simon Peter said, "You're the Christ, the Messiah, the Son of the living God."

Jesus came back, "God bless you, Simon, son of Jonah! You didn't get that answer out of books or from teachers. My Father in heaven, God himself, let you in on this secret of who I really am. And now I'm going to tell you who you are, really are. You are Peter, a rock. This is the rock on which I will put together my church, a church so expansive with energy that not even the gates of hell will be able to keep it out.

"And that's not all. You will have complete and free access to God's kingdom, keys to open any and every door: no more barriers between heaven and earth, earth and heaven. A yes on earth is yes in heaven. A no on earth is no in heaven." (16:15–19)

In this scene in Matthew, Jesus told Peter who he is and then used Peter's brand of faith to define the church. Later, when Peter wrote letters to the early church (1 and 2 Peter), he will tell all followers of Jesus who we are, who we *really* are. Let's look at one of those passages.

Read 1 Peter 2:4–5.
- What do these two verses teach you about Jesus? About yourself?
- How does Jesus' word to Peter in Matthew 16 inform Peter's word to all believers in 1 Peter?

Now the student has become the teacher. Peter has embraced his own chosenness and now he defines ours. First, he tells us that chosenness is a collective reality. We are chosen *together*. The *you* in this verse is plural, but every stone is chosen to fit with every other stone. Henri Nouwen wrote:

When we claim and constantly reclaim the truth of being the chosen ones, we soon discover within ourselves a deep desire to reveal to others their own chosenness. Instead of making us feel that we are better, more precious or valuable than others, our awareness of being chosen opens our eyes to the chosenness of others.[5]

The best way to live out our chosenness is by telling other people they can be chosen, too, but we won't do it if we don't first acknowledge our own chosenness—that God hasn't settled for you or me because nothing better came

THE MIRACLE OF CHOSENNESS

along. God *chose* us. God is not in a bad mood about us. He *loves* us. As with Jesus and Peter, God sees far more potential in us than we may see in ourselves. God sees us not just as we *are* but as we *can* be.

Do you remember the miracle story I told previously, about the woman whose blind eye was healed? Do you remember that the restoration of her sight was not her first miracle that weekend? At the retreat where I met her, she encountered the Holy Spirit in an inner healing moment. Her worthiness was revealed to her and she experienced instantaneous, miraculous freedom as God healed deep inner wounds. That's the miracle she went home with from the retreat. And out of that inner healing, physical healing happened.

Knowing ourselves as chosen? That's a miracle every time it happens. If you want to see miracles in your world, start by telling people about their chosenness. Then hang onto your socks, because the Holy Spirit is about to knock them off!

> Yes, Jesus sees your warts and imperfections, but he sees them as potential rather than shame.

LISTENING TO THE WORD

Write down everything you can think of that describes Jesus. For instance, the word *redeemer* is important to me in talking about Jesus; so is the word *anchor*. Now, write down all the things Jesus knows to be true about you. When you look at yourself from the perspective of Jesus, what do you see? Keep in mind that Jesus first of all sees you as chosen. He sees far more good in you than you see in yourself. Yes, Jesus sees your warts and imperfections, but he sees them as potential rather than shame. Ask the Holy Spirit to speak to you about who you are in Christ as you write. End with a prayer of thanksgiving for all God is forming in you.

9

WHAT YOU BELIEVE MATTERS

Key Observation.
To honor the heart of God is a profound calling.

> **Review three passages we've already looked at: Matthew 11:2–6, Luke 9:7–9, and Luke 9:18–20.**
> - Compare the motives of John the Baptist, Herod the Tetrarch, and Peter the apostle. What motivated John to ask Jesus if he was "the one"? (Matt. 11:20). What motivated Herod to wonder, "Who, then, is this I hear such things about?" (Luke 9:9). What motivated Jesus to ask his followers, "Who do you say I am?" (v. 20).
> - Why does it matter who Jesus is and who others say he is? Does it matter to you?

I'm thinking about a night years ago when a group of us went together to see the movie *The Passion of the Christ* when it first came out. Afterward we adjourned to my living room to discuss what we'd seen. In the midst of the dialogue, someone asked some kind of technical question about the way God works and someone else responded. Then a guy who happens to have been in professional ministry for some time made a comment that surprised me. He said, "Frankly, I don't have much use for theology. I just want to know who God is and what his heart is."

Correct me if I'm wrong, but isn't that pretty much the point of theology?

WHAT YOU BELIEVE MATTERS

"I don't have much use for theology." I bet that guy would have cared about my theology if we had been worshiping cows in my living room. It must be fun to sound like a renegade in a group of people talking about religion, but it can also be theologically dangerous. What you believe *matters*.

With limitless accessibility to the messages being preached by all kinds of rock-star preachers around the country, it is remarkably easy to get drunk on tweetable lines. We listen for cool people to say cool things, then we take the rest of it, hook, line, and sinker, without any sense of discernment. A little bit of the message of one rock-star preacher mixed with a bit of the message of another rock-star preacher, sprinkled with someone's cool comment on social media and before we know it, we're cooking up the theological equivalent of Cool Whip. A lot of light-weight fluff that tastes sweet but with little if any of the compelling, consistent gospel that leads directly into the heart of God.

Friends, hear me: what you believe matters.

This is what Christians believe: We believe Jesus is the hope of the world. We believe he is the way to life. *The way*. We believe he has defeated the power of sin and death, so we have nothing left to fear. *Nothing*. To carry a spirit of fear is to believe death still has power over our lives. Those who follow Jesus have nothing to do with fear (as Herod did) or with lies that make us live fearfully. We are not fearful people; we are hopeful people whose biggest questions about life and death have been answered.

> Our primary work as followers of Jesus is to honor the heart of God and live headlong into his values.

Followers of Jesus are called to represent the love of God among hurting people and to communicate through our lives the hope Jesus accomplished through the cross and empty tomb. We are the body of Christ on earth in this age. We share his values and his victory. When we choose the body of Christ as our identity, we set aside all rights to this world and submit to the values of the kingdom of God. We give everything to the service of those values.

Let me say that again another way: our primary work as followers of Jesus is to honor the heart of God and live headlong into his values.

That means that *everything*—our homes, families, funds, opinions—must submit to those values. We are no longer our own. We no longer get to live as we please, do as we please, say what we please. To the extent that we carry fear, anger, prejudice, unkindness, untruthfulness, discouragement, and selfishness, we compromise the body of Christ and deny our claims. How dangerous that is!

SUPERNATURAL

To the extent that we display faith, hope, and love, we honor the body of Christ.

God values the church. He loves his church because God loves people! People are not the problem; people are the prize! And the cross is our assurance of that truth. God has chosen every person who chooses Christ. God partners with people to carry out his purposes and for a reason that is far higher than my understanding, God has chosen *not* to carry out his purposes without us. Every action that flows from us, every opinion given, every decision made ought to be made with deepest humility in the face of such honor. God loves us and chooses us, and God gives us supernatural power and authority to join him where he is at work.

As the highest value and the purest love, as the hope of the world, Jesus Christ is worth my absolute, solemn devotion. Whatever I have to give up in the pursuit of more perfectly honoring this grace-filled, loving, creative God of the universe is worth it. He is worth my attention. He is worth my surrender. He is worth my trust. And he is worth the spiritual stretch toward living a truly supernatural life.

LISTENING TO THE WORD

Contemplate your identity as a chosen person, a royal priesthood. Meditate, word by word, phrase by phrase, on 1 Peter 2:9–10. Add the phrases that resonate to the list of statements you wrote down in an earlier chapter about who you are. And now, claim *this*: You are not a mistake or an afterthought or a life without meaning. You are *chosen*. Make a prayer of great thanksgiving for that life-giving fact.

10

THE GOSPEL OF WELCOME PART 1

Key Observation
Our job is to bless the people who let us in.

Read Luke 9:3–5.
- What are all the reasons you can think of that Jesus might have counseled his followers not to take anything for their journey?
- What might they have learned about the kingdom of God if they went out without stuff?
- Why do you suppose Jesus asked that they not move from house to house but stay in the first place that welcomed them?
- When it comes to the gospel of welcome, what distinguishes a "testimony against" from a "testimony for"? In other words, when does a welcome work against the gospel and when does it expose the glory of God?

There are few phrases that evoke more warmth or comfort than *Welcome home*. In that welcome, we experience all we need. We are safe. We are loved. We belong. This was the radical contribution made by first-century followers of Jesus. Their brand of religion was so much more than a set of rules. It was a people, a place, a family, and a purpose to which anyone could attach. This expression of faith in God exposed his heart for people. In the gospel of welcome, we remember that God is for us.

In Luke 9, the word *welcome* is used seven times in the New International Version. The first time we encounter the word in Luke 9, it is in the negative.

We're taught what to do when someone doesn't welcome us. Jesus gives clear instructions here for what to do when you're not welcomed into a place where you've gone specifically for the purpose of welcoming and exposing the kingdom of God. In short, he gives permission to move on. If the ground hasn't been plowed enough for seeds to take root, let it go. Let God do the work.

> **Rather than writing people off, our challenge is to cultivate a holy sensitivity to the spiritual readiness of others.**

In other words, Jesus is saying that our job is to bless the people who let us in. We have a message that has power to save lives. How anyone receives it is between them and God. Our job is simply to give what has been given to us. Jesus tells us clearly right here in Luke 9 that not everyone will accept a gift like that but some will. Our job is to keep tossing seeds and let God tend to the soil.

This is a word of reassurance for those of us who are tired and who just don't seem to have the strength to give anything more. Some of us have given and given and given, and we get nothing in return. To you, I offer a little encouragement from Luke 9: don't let your call to share the gospel ride on *your* circumstances, on *your* ego, or on *their* response. Let your call ride on the leading of the Holy Spirit.

Now, let's look for a moment at the word *dust*. Search "dust in the Bible" on the internet, and you'll find all kinds of articles. Dust is a popular topic in the kingdom of God! Where else besides Luke 9 do you find dust? How is dust related to life? What would it mean for you to "shake the dust off your feet" (Luke 9:5)?

Read Ecclesiastes 3:19–21.
- Take a few minutes to meditate on this passage, making notes about what is important to you in life. What does this verse say to you about the reality of life? What does it say about death?

By telling his followers to shake the dust from their feet when they left a town, Jesus seemed to be giving his followers permission to write folks off. And this line from Ecclesiastes may seem to make the same point. If life is dust, why bother? That might seem to be the message, but the big message of the Bible gives us a better framework to understand these passages. Rather than writing people off, our challenge is to cultivate a holy sensitivity to the spiritual readiness of others. Leave those who are reluctant to the care and timing of God. Don't hound or shame them. Life is too short for that. Instead, lean into those who are ready to receive the word and work of

THE GOSPEL OF WELCOME · PART 1

Christ. Who in your life is hungry for a word of encouragement? Who is ready to go to the next level of healing or spiritual formation? Who has welcomed you in for the sake of spiritual feeding? Invest your time there. Leave the rest to God's prevenient grace.

You may be thinking, *But what if I go and they do welcome me in, and then I don't know what to say? What if I end up sounding more like Mr. Christianese than myself?* I get it. If it helps, here are a couple of things I've learned over years of talking to folks about Jesus:

1. **If I feel uncomfortable, I can say so.** I just tell the person, "It isn't always easy for me to put my faith into words, but I do it because nothing has changed me more."

2. **I can use my own words.** I don't have to know all the right biblical terms or have all the right answers. I think one of the most powerful things you can say to someone is "I don't know." It lets them know you're real.

3. **I can leave the results to God.** My friend Bob Tuttle said it takes about twenty-five different witnesses before a real encounter with God takes place. If you are numbers one through twenty-four, you are just as important as number twenty-five. Until you give your witness, the next person can't give theirs. Let God be concerned with the results. Our job is simply to tell the story.

LISTENING TO THE WORD

Make a list of five people you can start praying for today. Ask God to give you a "holy welcome" in their life.

Group Gathering

OPEN WITH PRAYER

WATCH SESSION 2 VIDEO

DISCUSS THE FOLLOWING QUESTIONS BASED ON READINGS 6–10

6

Key Observation
It is a risky thing, but healthy, to step out into that mixture of doubt and faith, trusting like crazy he will show up and lead you through.

Question for Discussion
Where are you most likely to deal with feelings of doubt, and how are you learning to press through those feelings to bold expressions of faith?

7

Key Observation
What Jesus wants from every person who follows him is a clear witness.

Question for Discussion
How does the notion of a clear witness fit into the broader conversation about supernatural ministry?

8

Key Observation
In thinking about Peter's transformation from average disciple to eloquent apostle, we are invited to imagine the personal transformation that had to occur for Peter to stand confidently in this moment and profess this kind of faith.

Question for Discussion
When it comes to seeing ourselves as chosen, how does that encourage us in this journey of sanctification?

9

Key Observation
To honor the heart of God is a profound calling.

Question for Discussion
If this is our primary work, then what do we know about the heart of God by looking at the life of Jesus? And how does that knowledge translate into an active kind of honoring?

10

Key Observation
Our job is to bless the people who let us in.

Question for Discussion
How does the phrase "who let us in" affect your understanding of our job description as people called to bless others?

CLOSE WITH PRAYER

Perhaps the first welcome we need to learn is the welcome that invites the Holy Spirit into the room. Tonight, will you—along with your group—spend a few moments inviting the Holy Spirit into your midst? Invite him to speak wisdom where there have been questions. Invite him into any hard circumstances members of the group may be experiencing. Do not use this prayer time to instruct the Holy Spirit about what to do; simply invite the one who holds all power and authority into the room and into your lives.

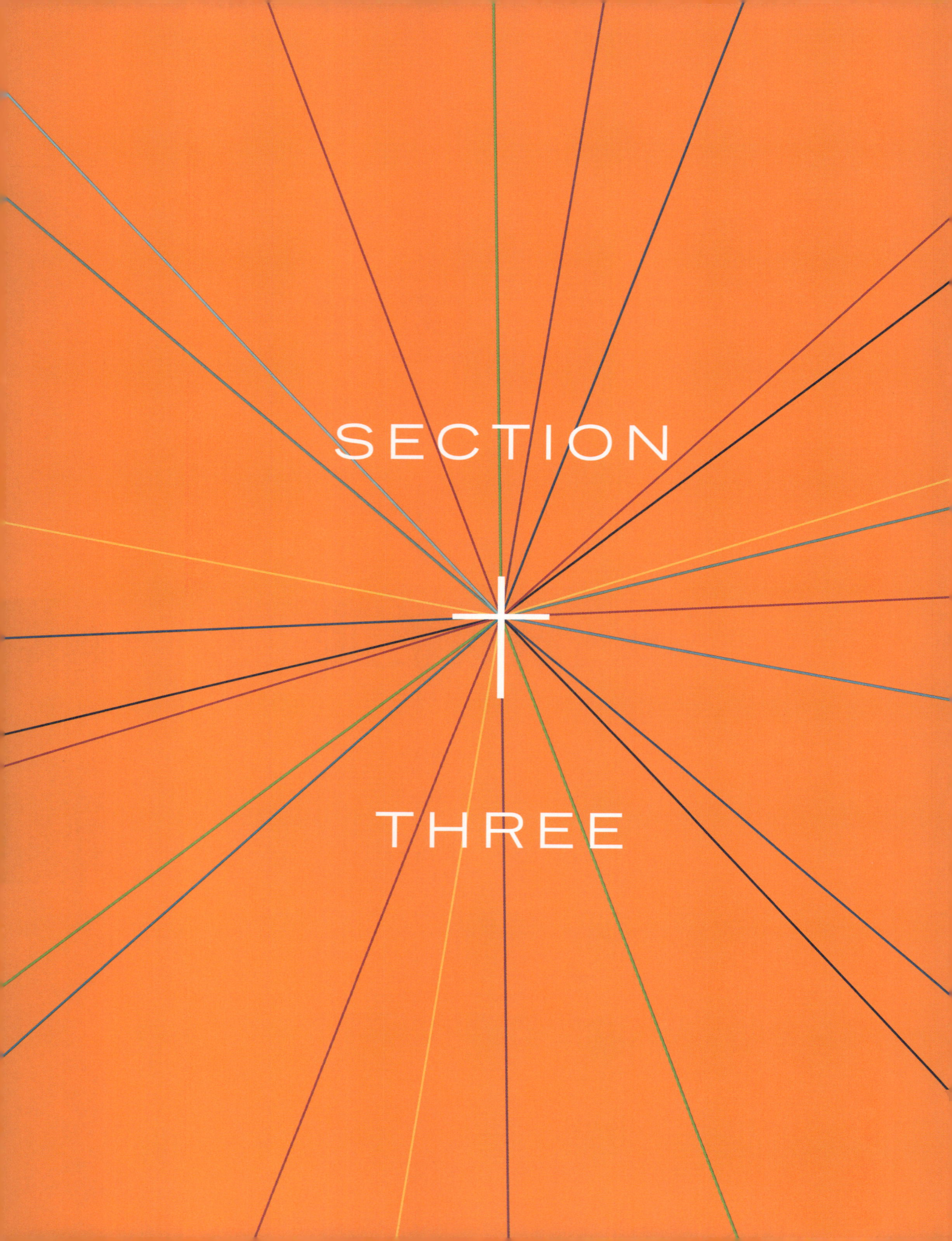

SECTION

THREE

11

THE GOSPEL OF WELCOME PART 2

Key Observation
We tend to get more riled up about the moments than the movement.

Read Luke 9:10–11.
- In Luke 9:1, Luke refers to the disciples as the Twelve. In Luke 9:10, he calls them apostles. Do you remember what the word "apostle" means? Why the shift in what he calls them?
- What is the nature of the "welcome" in this passage? Who is doing the welcoming? How does Jesus welcome people? Why did Luke include this point, that Jesus "welcomed them" (v. 11)?
- Think for a moment what it would feel like to experience a welcome from Jesus. What does his welcome include? What distinguishes a "Jesus welcome" from anyone else's welcome? How might this inform the way you welcome people into your home, your church, your small group, and your place of employment?

I know what you're thinking. You're thinking, *When are we going to get back to miracles and people passing out in worship and speaking in tongues and . . . you know, supernatural stuff?* I know you're thinking that because when I first got obsessed with Luke 9 and 10 that's what I was looking for. *Hey Luke, let's talk a little less about all this preparation and a little more about those seventy-two people and exactly how they healed, saved, and delivered! I want stories! Action! Let's see some people getting slain in the Spirit!*

SUPERNATURAL

Maybe that's not you. Maybe it was just me. But just in case, I want to challenge us both on this point. We tend to get more riled up about the moments than the movement leading up to them. We get excited about the fringe stuff and tend to discount all that has happened on the way to those moments.

Don't get me wrong, I'm not opposed to miracles and transformational moments. I'm all about them! And that's why I think this emphasis on the gospel of welcome in Luke 9 is so important. Because every person's salvation is a miracle story and every church should be cultivating more stories. A kingdom welcome necessarily includes an invitation to transformation. It is an invitation to receive the gospel, to receive healing, to receive deliverance. A true welcome is never just kindness or southern politeness or good marketing. A true welcome says, "We want you here just as you are, but we love you enough *not* to let you stay that way."

> A true welcome says, "We want you here just as you are, but we love you enough *not* to let you stay that way."

This seems a fitting description of how Jesus welcomed folks in. He didn't invite them in to find a place on the couch, nor did he expect them to go directly into the deep end of spiritual intimacy. Jesus welcomed folks in so they would no longer be strangers to the gospel. He invited them into his way of being, so he could expose them to kingdom things and offer healing to those who were receptive. Jesus' welcome assumed an invitation to encounter the in-breaking kingdom.

Remember that a true kingdom welcome invites someone into a supernatural experience that leads to life transformation—which means the results will outstrip the effort. And we will know it is the gospel and not just kindness when the results outstrip the effort.

Read John 20:21–22.
- What do you make of that greeting, "Peace be with you!" (v. 21). What is the significance of that greeting, coming just before Jesus breathed on them and imparted the Holy Spirit?
- Who sent Jesus? Who does Jesus send? Draw this on a page in your journal by showing the flow of "sent-ness" described in these verses. What does that image teach you? Who is the ultimate sender? To whom must you be connected if you are going to be sent?
- How does Jesus equip those whom he sends? How does this inform your reading of Luke 9:3–5, when Jesus told his followers not to take material possessions with them?

THE GOSPEL OF WELCOME · PART 2

In this passage, we encounter the "sent-ness" of Jesus and the "sent-ness" of his followers. "Sent-ness" is more than just going. It is going *under the power of the Holy Spirit*. I would argue that this applies also, and perhaps especially, to people who have been sent to greet folks at the door or sent into children's rooms to teach and lead. True "sent-ness" (as in, "God sent me to do this work") requires an infilling of the Holy Spirit. As we so often say at Mosaic, this is about hanging on to people way past good sense. It is the cultivation of a lavish, other-focused love that overflows in witness and compassion.

Likewise, a true kingdom welcome is driven by the power of the Holy Spirit because it is the Holy Spirit who teaches us to love and it is the Holy Spirit who ushers in healing and deliverance. The only way we can know we have God's brand of love is by receiving God's Spirit into our lives. Likewise, we will know we are filled with the Holy Spirit when we display the kind of supernatural love only God can inspire us to show.

The work of the Holy Spirit is to point us to Jesus and then to point us toward the world to welcome and advance the kingdom of God. Jesus said as much. The Holy Spirit does not exist primarily to give us a more satisfying worship experience. The Holy Spirit sends us into the world to love as Jesus loved, to welcome those who are ready to receive the gospel.

LISTENING TO THE WORD

The connection between Father and Son and between Son and disciple is worth our attention. Take a few moments to journal on that connection. How would a more intimate connection with the Father, through the Son, by the power of the Holy Spirit, impact the way you welcome others into your life? End this time of reflection by offering a prayer, asking God to give you that spirit of welcome.

12

LET'S EAT

Key Observation
When we watch for the in-breaking kingdom, we discover it is in fact breaking in all around.

Read Luke 9:10–17, then read John 6:32–40.
- How would you describe the disciples' attitude toward this big group of strangers?
- If you'd been one of those disciples, how would you have responded emotionally to Jesus' instruction in verse 13? Would it have felt like a challenge or more like a burden? Do you think any of the disciples saw the miracle coming?
- How does this moment and this charge compare with what we read earlier, about Jesus asking his followers not to take anything with them? What is the common denominator?
- What do you learn about the connection between faith and food from this story in Luke?
- How would you describe the connection between this story in Luke 9 and Jesus' teaching in John 6?

Jesus called himself the Bread of Life. In Luke 9, we encounter him being that in front of crowds of people. Then, as if to accentuate the point, he offered food to thousands of people in a field. That combination of spiritual welcome and practical hospitality is a powerful one-two punch. Many hearts have been opened and souls have been saved by the spread of a table along with the presentation of the gospel. Food brings people together. It makes the moment social. It helps us loosen up and appreciate one another. Food connects us. But in gospel terms, every table ought to lead to Christ.

LET'S EAT

In John 6:32–40, Jesus explained why offering the gospel is true spiritual food. He said, "I am the bread of life. Whoever comes to me will never go hungry, and whoever believes in me will never be thirsty" (v. 35). What a glorious promise.

In that way, this miracle of a massive meal in Luke 9 is something of a metaphor. There is Jesus, the Bread of Life himself, passing baskets of bread that refuse to run out. I'm struck by the thought that in a crowd that size there were surely a few folks who didn't quite catch what was happening. They didn't realize as they took bread from a neighbor and passed it on to someone else that every time bread was taken from a basket, somehow, miraculously, more bread appeared. The food never ran out. "Whoever comes to me will never go hungry" was literally being lived out on that hillside. Five thousand people ate from those loaves until they were full. Yet how many of them went home that day unchanged, because they had missed the miracle?

> In gospel terms, every table ought to lead to Christ.

Some time back, I got an e-mail from a guy who lives in another state—a person I know a little, but I don't really know. I had chatted with him maybe two or three times before. His e-mail began with something of an apology. He said he wasn't prone to receiving a word from the Lord, and was even less prone to passing such a thing along. Nonetheless, he'd gotten a word for my church (which he's never attended) and wanted me to have it. In his prayer time that morning, the Lord told him that someone at Mosaic was going to experience a miracle, probably sooner than later. Several times in the e-mail he repeated that this wasn't his usual thing but that he felt so strongly about what he heard that he thought he should pass it along.

At the time I received his e-mail, it happened that we as a church were in the middle of several situations. Some of our folks had things going on in their lives that could have used a miracle. I kind of wanted to use his e-mail like a gift card from God, something I could redeem for anything on my menu of needs. That's what I wanted to do, but evidently God doesn't work that way. Instead of redeeming a prophetic word for the miracle of my choosing, God had me wait and watch. I spent the rest of that month watching for where God might move among us.

During that month, I actually saw multiple moments of what I'd define as supernatural results. But maybe the biggest thing I noticed was how that e-mail changed my whole perspective. Because I was prompted by this guy's e-mail to watch for God, I became much more aware of the Holy Spirit at work among us.

When I *watched* for the kingdom of God to be exposed, I *saw* the kingdom of God exposed.

You see, whether my friend had sent that e-mail or not, we still would have received what God had purposed for us... but, *oh my!* What I might have missed if I hadn't been watching! What joy I've discovered in learning and applying this spiritual principle that when we watch for the breaking in of the kingdom, we discover it is in fact breaking in all around. The famous twentieth-century monk Thomas Merton said, "I have no program for this seeing. It is only given. But the gate of heaven is everywhere."[6] In other words, as much as we'd like someone to show us how to do this, this isn't the kind of thing we can figure out in a few easy steps. Spiritual eyesight is something we must pursue.

But there is a promise: if you will look for God, you will find him. Or maybe the better way to say it is that when we welcome God into our circumstances, God welcomes us into his kingdom.

LISTENING TO THE WORD

> How do you use food (meals, coffee, gifts, etc.) to welcome folks into a conversation about the kingdom of God? Whom can you invite to your table in the coming week? To whom can you offer a simple meal, some great conversation, maybe a healing touch, and the welcome of the good news about Jesus?

13

WHOM GOD PURSUES

Key Observation
The person we least want to welcome—into our community, into our homes, into our lives—is probably the person voted "Most Likely to Be Pursued" in the kingdom of God.

Read Luke 9:46–48.

- Luke 9:46 begins with an argument. What were the disciples arguing about? What might have prompted them to one-up one another on greatness?

- Take a moment to notice the spirit in which Jesus responded to his friends. Do you notice offense? Anger? Frustration? Or was Jesus simply making the most of a teachable moment?

- What does the word "welcome" mean in this context? What does the repetition teach you about what Jesus values?

- How does the concept of welcome answer the disciples' argument about greatness?

If you were making up a story to convince people of something, you'd want to make your story as compelling as possible. You'd want the players in the story to look really good, especially if you were trying to convince people of their believability. So when we find stories like this in the Bible, we have to assume that either: A) it really happened or, B) Luke was doing a crummy job of inventing a plotline.

I'm going with A.

SUPERNATURAL

Still, it is interesting to find scenes like this in the Bible. The writers (remember that the Bible is written by many different people, all inspired by one Holy Spirit) seem much more concerned with sharing the facts than with making things "look right," and this story is no exception.

> God has called us to love him and love others not just when we feel like it or when it is easy or when the other person is lovable—but all the time and especially when it is hard.

Reading this story in Luke 9, we don't get the sense that the disciples were arguing right in front of Jesus (at least they had that much sense), but eventually *everything* ends up in front of Jesus. He knew what they'd been discussing even if he hadn't heard them directly because he knew their hearts. Rather than taking a side (one does not get the sense that he was in the least bit offended by their talk), he found a child and set him in front of them. Jesus knew their competitive, self-justifying hearts, so he set this little boy right in the middle of their conversation. And he said, "Whoever welcomes this little child in my name welcomes me; and whoever welcomes me welcomes the one who sent me [God]" (v. 48). It is as if he was saying, "Okay, guys, make a mental note here. You don't have the same values as the kingdom so this won't sound logical to you, but the person you least want to welcome is the person *most likely being pursued by God*. And the time you least want to do it is probably the time God wants to use you."

Let that sink in. The person we least want to welcome—into our community, our homes, our lives—is probably the person voted "Most Likely to Be Pursued" in the kingdom of God. And God is most likely to call us to this work of welcome when we are least prepared for it.

It is interesting that the other later instance of the word *welcome* in Luke 9 happens at the expense of Jesus himself.

Read Luke 9:52–56.
- How did the disciples respond to this rejection? How did Jesus respond to this rejection? Which response sounds more familiar to you? What does Jesus' response teach you about God, about yourself, and about the world?

Let's recall who the Samaritans were. The Samaritans were the ones to be avoided at all costs by Jewish people. They were literally "the least, the last, and the lost." And while we now know that the least, last, and lost are the ones most likely to be pursued by God, first-century Jews didn't yet have that

WHOM GOD PURSUES

perspective. They only knew that their customs kept them from associating with Samaritans.

We can judge those first-century folks all day long, but the fact is that we also have our version of "Samaritans" in our lives. They are the people we hold a secret prejudice against. For me, it might be Florida fans and northerners (I'm a UGA graduate and a die-hard Georgian; don't judge me), or more seriously, people who don't fit into my socioeconomic status. Whoever those people are in your life who are not like us, we tend to brand, even if only subconsciously, as "not as good as us." And these "not as good as us" people were the very ones who refused to welcome Jesus' followers—the very same followers who'd just been arguing over who was the greatest. What irony!

While the disciples wanted to take offense at this slight, Jesus took none. In fact, he only took his own advice and moved on to another village. What he knew was that Samaritans were also the beloved of God. And he knew that while they might not be receptive to the gospel now, they'd be receptive eventually. Jesus understood kingdom timing, and he was willing to wait.

For Christians this is a crucial point. God has called us to love him and love others not just when we feel like it or when it is easy or when the other person is lovable—but all the time and especially when it is hard. We are called to love the Samaritans, the children, the socially awkward ones, the ones who don't look like us. We are never given permission to devalue others or send them to hell, even in our minds. That job does not belong to us. We are called to go beyond tolerance to even aspire to love perfectly from a pure heart.

Even the hard-to-love ones. Maybe especially them. Because everyone deserves to know themselves as pursued by God.

LISTENING TO THE WORD

Begin praying for this spirit of welcome to fall on your church. Remember, we're praying not just for southern politeness or generic kindness. We're praying for a supernatural ability to love even the least lovable ones. Pray for God to help you find your place in that welcome.

14

GATHERING A KINGDOM WELCOME

Key Observation
Until we have surrendered our heart—our prejudices, misconceptions, defenses, preferences—we won't pursue supernatural ministry.

- Look back over your notes from chapters 10 through 13 to answer the following questions: What major themes emerge? What new things have you learned about the gospel of welcome? What questions do you have? What new ideas are cropping up?

So far this week, we have learned what to do when we are not welcomed into a space for the sake of the kingdom (Luke 9:3–5). Then we learned about the radical welcome of Jesus (Luke 9:10–17). This isn't a picture of Jesus with a leper or Jesus loving on someone no one else likes. That time in verses 10 through 17 is a picture of Jesus making space for grace even when he was tired, even when his followers were tired. That informs and challenges me to have the kind of "welcome" in my spirit that doesn't falter when folks are on my last nerve (can I get an amen on that one?).

Later in Luke 9, there is a scene where the disciples are arguing over who is the greatest (Luke 9:46–48). This time, Jesus used the concept of welcome to teach his friends what kingdom greatness looks like. He challenged them to see people—really *see* them—as treasures in the kingdom of God.

Finally, we learned that even those the world calls outliers can be exclusive in their welcome (Luke 9:51–56). The Samaritans refused to welcome Jesus into their midst, missing the truth that this Jew was one who would die for

GATHERING A KINGDOM WELCOME

their sins. Yet, even here, Jesus was not offended. He knew that sometimes we have to step back and give the Holy Spirit room to work.

If we gather up all the uses of the word "welcome" in Luke 9, we get a 360-degree view of kingdom hospitality:

* Welcome people when you're tired.
* Welcome people when you're inconvenienced.
* Welcome people as a way of right-sizing your own ego.
* Welcome the ones you don't trust, don't like, or don't value.
* Welcome those who welcome you, and refuse to be offended by those who don't.

In summary, welcome people all the way through or as Peter would later write, learn to "love one another deeply, from the heart" (1 Peter 1:22).

> **Read 1 Peter 1:22–23.**
> * How does being born again figure into our ability to love deeply from the heart? How does being filled with the Holy Spirit figure into that ability?

Peter's wisdom is rich. Nowhere does he qualify our love for others by their behavior or response. He simply calls us to love deeply, and this is the very message we find in Luke 9 in all those instances where the word *welcome* shows up. It is a call to recognize that even when we get the welcome right, people on the receiving end of God's grace might not appreciate or even acknowledge it. Like the clueless ones who got a meal the day Jesus fed the five thousand, there will be people who take our welcome for granted. Sometimes the "Samaritan" won't return the kindness. Sometimes your close friends will fall into cycles of dysfunction they should be long past by now. Don't let that stop you from heading into the will of God. In other words, *don't let your welcome ride on their response.*

> Welcome others into your life not because they deserve it or are acting right but because Christ has welcomed you.

That may be something you need to hear this week. You may already be tired before your week has even started, and you just can't see any way you can give more than the minimum. Maybe you don't realize the problem is less about the other person's distastefulness and more about your ego. You may be oblivious to the callouses building on your heart toward those who matter most to God. And to you, however you find yourself today, Jesus would say: let your welcome ride on the leading of the Holy Spirit. Welcome others into your life not because they deserve it or are acting right but because Christ has welcomed you.

SUPERNATURAL

Let me let you in on a secret: until we have surrendered our heart—our prejudices, misconceptions, defenses, preferences—we won't pursue supernatural ministry. Until our hearts break for the ones who break God's heart, we won't get close enough to folks who need what only Jesus can offer. And yet, those folks are all around us. They are the couple whose marriage is falling apart. The woman whose depression binds her to her bed. The man whose pain has him buying oxycontin on the street. The dad whose recovery program isn't sticking. The mom who can't keep it bandaged together with memes and Bible verses. The child who is tired and cranky and spreading the pain. These are the ones who deserve a better gospel than what so much of Christianity has defaulted to. They *need* more than "tolerable." They are ripe for the breaking in of the kingdom, and the best gift we can give them is a genuine and radical welcome into that Spirit-filled world.

LISTENING TO THE WORD

I think of Hagar out there in the wilderness with her baby, kicked out by Sarah after she had slept with Abram, meeting "the One who sees me" (Gen. 16:13). And I think of the woman—my personal hero—who challenged Jesus when he told her his miracles were for the lost sheep of Israel: "Even dogs are allowed to eat the scraps that fall beneath their masters' table" (Matt. 15:27 NLT). That's what a kingdom welcome looks like. Pray for that. Cry out for it. Go after the capacity to see people—really *see* them—as they are. Right now, start praying for God to break your heart for people. Because I am absolutely convinced that broken hearts are what God uses to release miracles of healing and transformation into the world.

15

WHAT IT MEANS TO BE ALIVE

Key Observation
When we reach out our hands, lay them on someone, and call for the Holy Spirit to cast out a demon or cure a disease or heal what ails them, we are both calling out and pouring in.

Read Luke 9:23–25.

- "Whoever wants . . ." (v. 23). This is how Jesus began this challenge. What do you notice about those beginning words?
- How did Jesus describe the process of becoming a disciple (v. 23)? What must we do?
- Explain verse 24 in your own words. What do you think Jesus meant here when he said we can actually lose our life by trying to save it? What does this mean about the connection between surrender, faith, and life?
- Can you think of examples (without dishonoring anyone personally) of people who have "gained the world" but somehow still lost their purpose and identity? What factors seem to be more common among those who suffer this fate?

In this passage, Jesus is teaching us what it means to live, to *really* live. He shows us how followers are designed to live, and he connects following to surrendering. He warns us that by our refusal to surrender to the will of God, we may actually forfeit our access to true life. He asks us to consider the value of hanging onto the values of this world at the cost of our very identity and purpose.

These are powerful words from Christ himself about what it means to live fully—to be completely and wholly alive. This is a theme that runs throughout

SUPERNATURAL

Scripture. Leviticus, which must be the most misunderstood book of the Bible, carries the key to the whole story of God because Leviticus in one word is about life (it is also about holiness but I would contend that holiness is the good life, and a call to "be holy as I am" is a call to abundant living).

In fact, Leviticus is about as relevant a life lesson as it gets. Moses, the writer of Leviticus and the leader of the Israelite people, became a master at human nature as he helped a group of people navigate their options. And at the end of a decades-long journey together, Moses boiled all the choices of his people down to just two: life or death. In Leviticus, Moses teaches us that while there may seem to be countless options, there are really only these two.

> I can say with absolute authority that there is nothing in Luke 9 about dispensing the power of the Holy Spirit with an eyedropper. So go after the fullness of the Holy Spirit.

Why did Moses have to teach the Israelites what it means to live? Dennis Prager, a Jewish man, has written extensively on this topic of life and death in the Israelite worldview. He talked about the Egyptian's preoccupation with death; their bible was called the Book of the Dead. Their greatest monuments were pyramids, which were basically oversized caskets. As pagans, the Egyptians were everything the kingdom of God was not. So when God brought the Israelite people up out of slavery from Egypt, he had to totally reorient their thinking. Hundreds of years of wrong theology had to be dismantled. The work in the desert was the work of learning to live. So the book of Leviticus, which has to be the most misunderstood book in the Bible, is actually all about life. What we eat, what we wear and watch and get entertained by, who we choose for intimacy—all those rules in Leviticus that sound like they are sucking the fun out of life are actually about rejecting the culture of death imposed by the Egyptians so that God's chosen people could choose life in every detail of living it.

If this is a fair interpretation, then in Luke 9, Jesus was just paraphrasing Leviticus. And when Leviticus teaches the Jews to rid their houses of every speck of yeast, maybe that is God helping his people rehearse for the days of Luke 9 when Jesus sent his followers out with power and authority to look for signs of death, signs of Egypt, signs of the anti-kingdom. And he essentially told them, "Wherever you see them—demons, disease, sickness—cast out death and proclaim life over my people. You are being sent out to claim victory over the culture of death. Go out there, swimming in the Holy Spirit, claiming your authority to choose life."

Jesus came that we might have life and have it to the full. When we reach out our hands, lay them on someone, and call for the Holy Spirit to cast out a demon or cure a disease or heal what ails them, we are both calling out and pouring in. We are calling out death and pouring in life.

> ### Read John 6:63 and John 7:38.
> - What do you learn from these two verses about the relationship between the Holy Spirit and life?
> - How does this change your thinking about the value of life?
> - How does it change your thinking about the centrality of the Holy Spirit in the life of faith?

Folks, the Holy Spirit breeds life into ministry. Go after the Holy Spirit. Ask God to pour out his Spirit over you—lavishly. I can say with absolute authority that there is nothing in Luke 9 about dispensing the power of the Holy Spirit with an eyedropper. So go after the fullness of the Holy Spirit. The *whole* gospel. Don't settle for anything less, because anything less is not Luke 9 living.

LISTENING TO THE WORD

Christ is your life, not your stuff, not your job, not your people, not your education. If this is true, then everything—every single thing—in your life leads to either life or death. What in your life breeds the spirit of death? And what in your life breeds the spirit of life? Spend time in the presence of God taking a spiritual inventory of your life. Ask the Lord to help you acknowledge those habits and hang-ups that breed death in you. Then commit to a season of repentance that allows you to be set free from those things.

Group Gathering

OPEN WITH PRAYER

WATCH SESSION 3 VIDEO

DISCUSS THE FOLLOWING QUESTIONS BASED ON READINGS 11–15

11

Key Observation
We tend to get more riled up about the moments than the movement.

Question for Discussion
In shaping a fresh understanding of supernatural ministry, what is the difference between going after moments and going after movement?

12

Key Observation
When we watch for the in-breaking kingdom, we discover it is in fact breaking in all around.

Question for Discussion
How have you experienced the in-breaking kingdom—in small daily blessings? In profound moves of God? What is the difference? Would both be considered as supernatural moves in your opinion?

13

Key Observation
The person we least want to welcome—into our community, into our homes, into our lives—is probably the person voted "Most Likely to Be Pursued" in the kingdom of God.

Question for Discussion
Without naming them for your group (because that might not be the kindest thing), who might God have put directly in your life because he is using you in his pursuit of them in a supernatural way? And how does that thought change your perspective?

14

Key Observation
Until we have surrendered our heart—our prejudices, misconceptions, defenses, preferences—we won't pursue supernatural ministry.

Question for Discussion
Is it possible to access the supernatural power of God without a surrendered heart?

15

Key Observation
When we reach out our hands, lay them on someone, and call for the Holy Spirit to cast out a demon or cure a disease or heal what ails them, we are both calling out and pouring in.

Question for Discussion
How would you say that our value of life (and our definition of it) affects our pursuit of supernatural ministry?

CLOSE WITH PRAYER

Close this session by practicing the value of life. As a group, lay hands on anyone in the room who is dealing with illness, whether physical, spiritual, or emotional. Invite one or more people in the circle to lead that prayer. Pray also over those in your circles of influence who are dead to Christ, seeking God's spiritual healing over their lives that they might live . . . *truly* live!

SECTION

FOUR

SURRENDER AND THE SUPERNATURAL

Key Observation
In order to enter into the miraculous works of God, we have to let go of self and begin to see the world from God's perspective. This is God's work, God's job.

Read Luke 9:23.

- What three personal choices, according to verse 23, must be present in order for a person to be a disciple of Christ?
- Describe what these choices look like in a life. What does it mean to deny oneself? What does it mean to take up one's cross? What does it mean to follow Jesus?

Deny yourself and *take up your cross* are detachment terms. Jesus is asking us to let go of life as we know it.

To deny yourself is to detach from self-interest. This is completely counterintuitive for fallen human beings. The survival instinct built into our biology prompts us to protect ourselves. We tend to pull back and find our protective crouch, not always on the front end but certainly at the point where it gets risky.

Self-protection—as in, protecting your own self-interests—centers on one key word: *self*. It is the Enemy's first line of defense. He doesn't care if I love myself too much or hate myself even a little; either end of that spectrum works.

In either case, my mental posture will keep me focused on *self*, which means I will have less room or maybe even no room for God.

In order to enter into miraculous works of God, we have to let go of ourselves and begin to see the world from God's perspective.

I'm thinking about Moses (okay, I'm *always* thinking about Moses because I love his story). When he first talks to God about what it would be like for him to become a redeemer for Israel, the one who would lead them out of slavery, Moses started with himself (see Exodus 4:1–17). He told God, "I can't do this. I'm not bold. I don't talk so good. I'm not cut out for this kind of thing." These are self-doubting and self-protecting arguments. God responded to that by saying, in my own paraphrase, "You're right. You can't do this, not on your strength. But you can do this on *my* strength."

Then God told him to take his staff and throw it down on the ground. When he does, it becomes a snake. That's a nifty little trick. But God doesn't stop there. He then asks Moses to pick up the snake again, by its tail. When Moses does this, it becomes a staff again.

If I were Moses, my problem in this scene would not be with throwing a staff on the ground to watch it turn into a snake. My problem would be with picking up the snake it had become. And that ends up being quite the point where "denying self" is concerned. For many of us, the real test isn't what we have to lay down; the real test is what we pick up in its place. Too often, we just swap one bad habit for another, but Jesus doesn't teach that here in Luke 9. Instead, when I lay my own life down, am I willing to deny myself and take up the life Christ has for me, trusting that his life is better than anything I might choose for myself?

In Luke 9:23, when Jesus is telling us to deny self, the key word here is not *deny* but *self*. This is about focus. One of our team members says that in her studies, she learned that "to deny myself means to deny my own lordship. My focus moves from me to Jesus. It doesn't mean to deny my feelings, my happiness, or my sense of worth. And to be honest, if I don't find happiness, worth, and joy in following Jesus, then I'm doing it wrong."

But don't we want all want ourselves to survive? Of course, but we're not the ones who can make that happen. Ultimately, that is God's job. *The Message* version of Ephesians 2:8–9 puts it this way: "Saving is all his idea, and all his work. All we do is trust him enough to let him do it. It's God's gift from start to finish! We don't play the major role. If we did, we'd probably go around bragging that we'd done the whole thing!"

SURRENDER AND THE SUPERNATURAL

Moses needed that staff trick to remind himself that this work he'd been given was not about him. Not at all. In order to enter into miraculous works of God, we have to let go of ourselves and begin to see the world from God's perspective. This is God's work, God's job.

My worst responses will be at the point of my believing that I am the one responsible for my own salvation, identity, or happiness. In the sense that I must choose Christ, I am responsible. But in the sense that I can keep my hands on all the controls once that choice is made, I'm not. Because here's the thing. Redemption doesn't work if I try to attach strings to my terms of surrender. It only works when I freely and unconditionally give up my right to self-ownership.

Folks, this is the cost of discipleship—the surrender of our rights to our own lives. Until we are ready to make that exchange, the redemption isn't "free and clear." But hear the good news: The gift on the other side of surrender unto death is an invitation to eternal, abundant, and adventurous *supernatural* life.

LISTENING TO THE WORD

In what area of your life do you need to loosen up and let go of control? Or where in your life are you practicing self-protectiveness instead of surrender? Make some notes about that right now, then create a prayer in response, asking God to give you courage to let him have those things that create anxiety in your life.

17

I AM THE GOD WHO HEALS YOU

Key Observation
If we will surrender our own perspective and allow him to live in us, we will become more effective as followers, as people.

Read Luke 9:23 again.
- Jesus qualifies the part about taking up our cross. Why do you suppose he threw in the word "daily"?
- Meditate on the phrase "take up their cross daily," and write anything that comes to mind. Then make that phrase into a personal prayer for the day: "Lord, help me to take up my cross today."

Crosses were a sick, extreme form of torture borrowed by the Greeks and Romans from the Phoenicians. The cross on which Jesus hung was a foreign thing. Which means that Jesus is asking his followers to learn how to pick up things that are foreign to them, that seem unnatural. In fact, he is asking us to pick up things that seem out of character for us, that friends from high school would not recognize as our normal. The very things that might have seemed foreign to us before we chose to follow Jesus are the very things that qualify us as followers of Jesus now.

But Jesus doesn't ask us to pick up our cross just once. He calls us to take up our cross *daily*. Why? Because Jesus isn't interested in arresting our development. This is an invitation to learn how to "adult," which flies in the face of so much that comes at us from every other direction. Our culture encourages us to pander to our inner child, which causes us to spend far more time accommodating the child we used to be (by protecting and hiding) than encouraging the adult we can become.

He is asking us to take up a new normal and to keep on practicing that new normal until it becomes who we are. Folks, this is a fact: Jesus intends to kill you. In a good way.

> ### Read Luke 9:24–25.
> - What would saving one's own life look like for a first-century follower of Jesus? Is Jesus speaking figuratively here (remember his original audience) or literally?
> - Who would have been their cultural examples of people who had gained the whole world? How would they have viewed those examples? Would they have admired them or been suspicious of them?
> - Now that you've read this passage over the shoulders of its original audience, paraphrase it for today's audience. How would you interpret this passage for today?

Here is how I would summarize these two verses: to get to this promise of new life, something has to die. This was a recurring theme in Jesus' teachings, and in fact is already a recurring theme in this study. In a similar teaching in John 12, Jesus, talking about his own death, told his followers, "Unless a kernel of wheat falls to the ground and dies, it remains only a single seed. But if it dies, it produces many seeds. Anyone who loves their life will lose it, while anyone who hates their life in this world will keep it for eternal life" (vv. 24–25). This context helps us understand more about what our willingness to give up this life means. It means, first of all, that we will bear more spiritual fruit if we let go of our incessant need to control everything and protect ourselves.

> Jesus is saying that his choice for how we live is always going to be better than our choice for how we live.

Let that sink in. It is completely counterintuitive for most of us but is what Jesus teaches. If we will surrender our own perspective and allow him to live in us, we will become more effective as his followers, as people. Sometimes we have to let the old die so that we'll be motivated to move on to more fruit.

Second, it means that what seems like giving up life is actually a trade-off for an assurance of eternal life. The word *eschaton* refers to the final event in the divine plan. The final event in God's plan is the ultimate defeat of the Enemy of your soul and the renewal of the world he created. The final event is the death of death and of everything that isn't fit for the kingdom of God.

When God says to people living in exile, "I know the plans I have for you . . . plans to prosper you and not to harm you, plans to give you hope and a future" (Jer. 29:11), he is not playing around with whether or not we have a good day. He is saying that he has the power to determine our future because he knows how we are made. Jesus is saying that *his* choice for how we live is always going to be better than *our* choice for how we live.

Because Jesus has broken the power of sin and death, his return is guaranteed and his victory is a done deal. Jesus now defines life. In order to get to *real* life, we claim Jesus as life, then we detach from our idols, die to our self, and let Jesus take up residence in our being. We tabernacle (house) this life of Jesus in our bodies. That is how we become the church—invested with the same power and authority Jesus had, who cast out demons, cured diseases, proclaimed the kingdom, and healed the sick.

This was true in the first century when Jesus walked the earth, and it is true today. Christ is your life. When you give up your life in favor of his, this becomes your hope of glory and your pathway into the supernatural realm . . . where the living is good.

LISTENING TO THE WORD

> In what areas of your life do you need to pray for freedom? Where are you holding onto the old life and resisting the invitation into something new? Don't think only about your personal junk. Think also about old and ineffective ways of following Jesus. In what ways are you practicing Christianity without power? Do you need to repent of that?

18

WHAT ABOUT MANIFESTATIONS?

Key Observation

While I am an enthusiastic believer of experiences that build personal faith, I do believe the emphasis when it comes to the anointing of the Holy Spirit is on building the kingdom of God on earth.

Read Luke 9:1–62.

- Underline any words, phrases, or sentences that seem to indicate an experience that is more supernatural than natural. For instance, casting out a demon is more supernatural, while teaching is more of a natural ability.
- Count the number of people in this chapter, then count the number of people who encountered something supernatural in the course of living as followers (or recipients) of Jesus' ministry.

Read 1 Corinthians 12:7–11.

- Why are these manifestations given (see v. 7)?
- Read through this list of supernatural giftings again. In what way are all these various giftings similar?
- Which of these giftings or manifestations do you think were at work among the disciples in Luke 9 as they went out under the power of the Holy Spirit to cast out demons, cure diseases, proclaim the kingdom, and heal the sick?

At this point, it seems appropriate to think about the difference between the anointing of the Lord for supernatural ministry and the kinds of spiritual manifestations that often accompany passionate encounters with Jesus Christ through the Holy Spirit.

Paul described to the Corinthian church the kind of empowerment—what we might call spiritual gifts—that seems to accompany those who follow Jesus and are filled with the Holy Spirit. Paul said these gifts are given "for the common good" (v. 7). Not for bragging rights. Not to make our quiet times more exciting. These gifts are for proclaiming the kingdom, and they are varied so we will learn to depend on one another and build on one another's strengths.

Can we take a moment here to remember that gifts and manifestations of the Spirit are not for the few, the deep, the weird . . . the *others*. According to Scripture, having spiritual gifts is what it means to live a rich, full life. It means being filled with the Holy Spirit! The Holy Spirit is our inheritance. If you call yourself a child of God, he belongs to you and you belong to him. You're his kid. It is his pleasure to give himself to us (see Luke 11:13). We don't have to beg or wonder. And we don't have to resist because his gifts are *always* good, even the ones that take us to the edge of our comforts.

God wants to empower his people so we can participate in the building of his kingdom on earth. He gifts us for partnership. Remember that. We'll come back to it.

> Our faith is not primarily individualistic. It is primarily about our partnership with God "for the common good."

But how do the gifts of the Spirit that build up ministries and extend the kingdom of God differ from more personal manifestations, such as being overcome by the Holy Spirit in worship or receiving a language from heaven? Here's how I'd define the difference: spiritual gifts build up the faith of others, while manifestations build up *your* faith. Notice the common theme? Faith! When these kinds of experiences show up in the Bible—stories of someone having a vision or being caught up into heaven or experiencing great joy or great revelation—the writer is usually talking about something happening on the spiritual plane that activates a new level of faith.

That's what happened to Paul on the road to Damascus. His very deep, personal, and convicting encounter with the risen Jesus accomplished a very deep, personal result. That is the effect of a spiritual manifestation. When it is received by a mature, surrendered heart, it accomplishes deep, spiritual things and it results in greater faith. That's why we ought to keep an open heart toward these mysteries. Because . . . *faith*.

And while I am an enthusiastic believer of experiences that build personal faith, I do believe the emphasis of the anointing of the Holy Spirit should be on building the kingdom of God on earth. In other words, I believe there is a caution here about emphasizing the deeply personal experiences to the exclusion of the very public, bold, and kingdom-building ones. In other words, be careful not to reduce all spiritual encounters to only the "good feels" they produce in your personal worship time with God. Our faith is not primarily individualistic. It is primarily about our partnership with God "for the common good." We are called to make disciples and build up the body of Christ. That's God's heart. Use your spiritual gifts to *make disciples*. Use your personal experiences with the Holy Spirit to build your faith so you can *make disciples*.

In his journal, John Wesley said, concerning manifestations, that the danger is not to regard them too much but to regard them too little. He cautioned against too much skepticism. "It is not wise to give up this part, any more than to give up the whole." Wesley would say God is often present precisely at the point of the mystery. He wrote of first-person experiences of those who "suddenly and strongly" found themselves convinced of sin, "the natural consequence whereof were sudden outcries and strong bodily convulsions.... [God] favored several of them with divine dreams, others with trances and visions."[7] Early Methodism was characterized by the experience of God's transforming supernatural power.

Are the things we encounter in the Spirit sometimes contrived? Yes. Are they sometimes forced? Sure. And, sometimes, people are genuinely filled and empowered to do and experience beautifully powerful supernatural things. I am convinced God wants to do far more in and through us than we could imagine for ourselves. The Bible tells me so (see Ephesians 3:20). And every time God surprises me with more, the Spirit witnesses to my spirit that I am a child of the one, true God. And I rejoice!

LISTENING TO THE WORD

Write all your doubts, fears, and questions as a prayer to the living God, and then surrender them to him. Don't attempt to answer them yourself. Just surrender them to the God who hears you.

19

AWAKENED

Key Observation
The collective witness and teaching of the Scriptures tell me that dreams, vision, and the voice of God can be expected of those who are fully awake to God's movements on earth.

Read Luke 9:28–32.
- Imagine the sensory experience of this transfiguration. Make notes of the sight and feel of it, the sounds, the smells. What strikes you as most powerful?
- When the disciples talked about this moment later, what do you think they remembered most?

This scene makes me hungry for heaven. Jesus had just been talking with his followers about the connection between his glory and their faith, and then he headed up a mountain to pray with Peter, James, and John. As he was praying, the appearance of his face changed and his clothes became as bright as a flash of lightning. Two men, Moses and Elijah, appeared in glorious splendor to talk with Jesus. They spoke about his departure from this earth, among other things. Peter, James, and John are sleepy, but the story says, "When they became fully awake, they saw his glory" (Luke 9:32).

"When they became fully awake, they saw his glory." Meditate on that line for a moment, then ask yourself: *If I am not seeing God's glory, is it because God's glory is absent or is it because (spiritually speaking) I am slogging through life half asleep?*

I had just finished speaking at a memorial service when a man, who I had not met before, walked right up and said, "I know just what you were talking about up there. I couldn't hear a word you said, even though I have my hearing aids in (at which point his wife said, "But no batteries"), but I know exactly what you're talking about. I have been there. I have seen him."

I asked, "Seen who?"

"Jesus."

"Really? You saw Jesus? For real?"

"Yes. Eight years ago, I died in a car accident. The medic cut a hole between my ribs and stuck an oxygen tube into my collapsed lungs, and I died. Jesus met me. I didn't see his face, but I know it was him because I saw the holes in his hands. I have seen things we can't even imagine on earth."

"Like what?" I said, because I've just preached a funeral and times like that, these conversations seem less crazy and more relevant. I'm not about to let him go without finding out what he has seen.

"I saw a light," he said, beaming, "that was about ten times brighter than the sun, but it didn't hurt your eyes to look at it. You know how you can't look directly into the sun? Well, you can look directly at this light, but it doesn't hurt. And it was golden. It was the most beautiful thing I have ever seen."

"Did you see any other people?"

"There was one person at the end of the tunnel."

"Who was it?"

"I don't know. I never got there." And then he waved his hand in the air as if directing someone to turn around, and he said, "Jesus sent me back here before I got to the end of the tunnel."

"Why do you suppose you got sent back?"

> If I am not seeing God's glory, is it because God's glory is absent or is it because (spiritually speaking) I am slogging through life half asleep?

"He didn't say, but I think it was because my mother was sick and needed me to care for her. I can tell you this: I can't wait to go back. I have absolutely no fear of death now. It is so beautiful."

I stood there in the doorway of that little chapel and let that conversation sink in. I looked at that man who seemed to glow with faith, and I let the truth of heaven wash over me. I wondered to myself: *How many normal, everyday, average people have died from heart attacks and snake bites and allergic reactions, only to see Jesus and taste that golden light before being sent back here to live another*

SUPERNATURAL

life? How many have seen those hands with holes in them? How many have been handed the gift of assurance in the form of a car crash they didn't survive, then did? I suspect it's more than we think. As Thomas Merton said, "The gate of heaven is everywhere."[8] How would I react if I died and went to heaven and then lived to talk about it? Perhaps more relevant is this question: Would I recognize it if heaven came to me?

There are some powerful scenes in the Bible of God showing up in front of people. Abraham was escorted by the voice of God out into the night and told he would have as many children as stars in the sky. Moses was drawn to a bush that wouldn't stop burning, only to hear God say, "Take off your sandals, for the place where you are standing is holy ground" (Ex. 3:5). Isaiah and Ezekiel were both transformed by visions in which they were taken up into heaven. Paul spoke about his own experience of being taken up into heaven to see things he couldn't describe. John, the author of Revelation, was the audience of the most extensive and powerful vision of the world to come.

We could go on and on. The collective witness and teaching of Scripture tells me that dreams, visions, and the voice of God can be expected of those who are fully awake to God's movements on earth. I encourage you to take time right now to cry out to God for dreams, visions, and his voice—for a supernatural experience of the Christian life. As Peter, James, and John discovered, that experience will put you in the company of greatness.

LISTENING TO THE WORD

"When they became fully awake, they saw his glory." I challenge you to develop that kind of eyesight that can see corners of the kingdom exposed for our benefit and pleasure and to build our faith and prove again that what we talk about is true. Look for signs today, then spend at least ten minutes tonight reflecting on or writing about what you saw.

20

CHECK YOUR LIFE

Key Observation
*Do you fully own the fact that you believe in a supernatural
God who is more than capable of supernatural things?*

> ### Read Luke 9:28–32 again.
> - Why do you think Jesus chose Peter, James, and John. Why them? Why not three other guys (or women) who were following him?
> - List everything you know about these three disciples. Why do you suppose they were in the inner circle?
> - Why do you think this scene happened?
> - Who was helped by it, or what purpose did it serve in the story of Jesus?

I once polled friends on Facebook to find out what they considered to be the biggest sins of middle-class, twenty-first-century America. Answers ranged from entitlement (the most popular response), fear, and jealousy to instant gratification and self-deception (trying to convince ourselves that we as individuals are more valuable than those around us). Two other sins listed were on two ends of a spectrum: active anger on one side, and passivity or sloth (which is in the list of the seven deadly sins) on the other.

Passivity is a kind of disconnection that leads to a lack of passion or compassion. For the record, Jesus was not a fan. The resurrected Jesus, in Revelation 3:16, condemned those who were neither hot nor cold. "Because you are lukewarm . . . I am about to spit you out of my mouth." It is not an enviable place to be.

During one of the great spiritual awakenings of the last several hundred years, continued passion and sustainable faith was a major concern. During the

SUPERNATURAL

Methodist revival of the eighteenth century, John Wesley was more interested in raising up Christians with authentic faith than with having large numbers in attendance. Indeed, passivity and being lukewarm were the most common reasons for which John Wesley removed people from the Methodist roll. The offending grievance was "lightness and carelessness."[9] What this revivalist could not tolerate was casual and disconnected observation. Such casual faith was not abided in the eighteenth century any more than it could be abided in the first-century church. To be Methodist during the Great Awakening meant to be devoted to the apostle's teaching and to fellowship, to the breaking of bread and to prayer. Attendance at class meetings—a form of community discipleship—was a requirement. To be Methodist was to be alive to the Spirit at work in the community. In other words, what the Methodists earnestly desired was to be plain, scriptural Christians.

More recent studies tell a different story about the people of God. Active attendance in church today is defined as attending three out of eight Sundays. This reflects a growing trend away from church as the gathering place for spiritually alive followers of Jesus, and it highlights our collective passivity toward the things of God.

The sin of passivity seems to sneak up on us from behind. Overstimulated by so much aggression and so many words, we shut down our feelings just to cope. We find ourselves disappearing in binge-sessions of *NCIS* (preaching to myself here) or, worse yet, reality TV (where we can feel better about ourselves because at least we're not *them*).

> Do you fully own the fact that you believe in a supernatural God who is more than capable of supernatural things?

I bring this up *not* because I suspect the disciples in this story in Luke 9 were guilty of sloth. I bring it up because often we notice that the disciples were either not completely awakened to the things of God or they were startled by them. They seemed to forget that they had a supernatural Messiah seated in the heavenly places with the Father, even as he walked on earth. And that in fact they, too, are seated in heaven, in some supernatural way that can't quite be explained (see Ephesians 2:6–7).

This scene is one of those times. Half asleep, these disciples (who were in his inner circle; don't miss that point) were startled to discover Jesus socializing with Moses and Elijah. When they realized what was happening right there in their midst, they roused to a more awakened spiritual place.

CHECK YOUR LIFE

> **Read Luke 9:32–36.**
> - What do you suppose motivated Peter to speak?
> - Do you recall a cloud anywhere else in the Bible, especially one indicating the presence of God? (Hint: Read Exodus 40.)

By Peter's comments, it is obvious that they still didn't completely comprehend how they should absorb this, but there they were, privy to one of the most supernatural moments in their whole journey with Jesus. In the South, we have an ironic saying: "Bless your heart." It is what we say when someone doesn't quite get it right. In this scene, Peter was having a "bless your heart" moment, but can you blame him? Would you do any better, if you were the one trying to make sense of this supernatural scene? I can only imagine that from that day forward, those three followers of Jesus must have been so hungry for heaven, so much more awake to the in-breaking kingdom around them. Because once you've seen it, you can't unsee it.

Do you ever wonder what you may have missed because you were not fully awake to the glory of God? How many moments have there been when the Holy Spirit showed up on your doorstep, urging you forward in your spiritual life, and you missed it because you weren't all in? Do you fully own the fact that you believe in a supernatural God who is *more than capable* of supernatural things? Do you own the fact that you, also, are seated with him in heaven—right now? The kingdom of heaven is indeed real, and we have witnesses to that fact. Oh, that we might have eyes to see it too.

LISTENING TO THE WORD

> What kind of prayer do these truths evoke? My friends, we ought all be praying for more faith, more love, and more power to live what God has revealed to us. Take time now to pray for the quality and quantity of your faith.

Group Gathering

OPEN WITH PRAYER

WATCH SESSION 4 VIDEO

DISCUSS THE FOLLOWING QUESTIONS BASED ON READINGS 16–20

16

Key Observation
In order to enter into the miraculous works of God, we have to let go of self and begin to see the world from God's perspective. This is God's work, God's job.

Question for Discussion
How does it ease your mind (or stir it) to hear that Spirit-empowered ministry is more about surrender than self or self-effort?

17

Key Observation
If we will surrender our own perspective and allow him to live in us, we will become more effective as followers, as people.

Question for Discussion
How might God be drawing you into a new perspective about following Jesus, and what perspective/bias might you need to confess and relinquish in order to make room for something new?

18

Key Observation
While I am an enthusiastic believer of experiences that build personal faith, I do believe the emphasis when it comes to the anointing of the Holy Spirit is on building the kingdom of God on earth.

Question for Discussion
With that perspective in mind, what do you notice about the miracles in Luke 9? Were they primarily for the sake of the individual, or primarily for the sake of building the kingdom?

19

Key Observation
The collective witness and teaching of the Scriptures tell me that dreams, vision, and the voice of God can be expected of those who are fully awake to God's movements on earth.

Question for Discussion
What has been your experience with dreams, visions, and the voice of God?

20

Key Observation
Do you fully own the fact that you believe in a supernatural God who is more than capable of supernatural things?

Question for Discussion
Reread the question found in the key observation for this day. Do some soul searching around this one: Do you fully own the fact that you believe in a supernatural God who is more than capable of supernatural things?

CLOSE WITH PRAYER

Invite the group to pray for faith in the supernatural power of God. Pray aloud so each member of the group can agree with others as each prays for the Holy Spirit to make the things of the kingdom more real to us than things of this world. Pray for hunger. Pray for boldness. Pray for God's kingdom to come on earth just as it is in heaven . . . and pray that it would come *through you*.

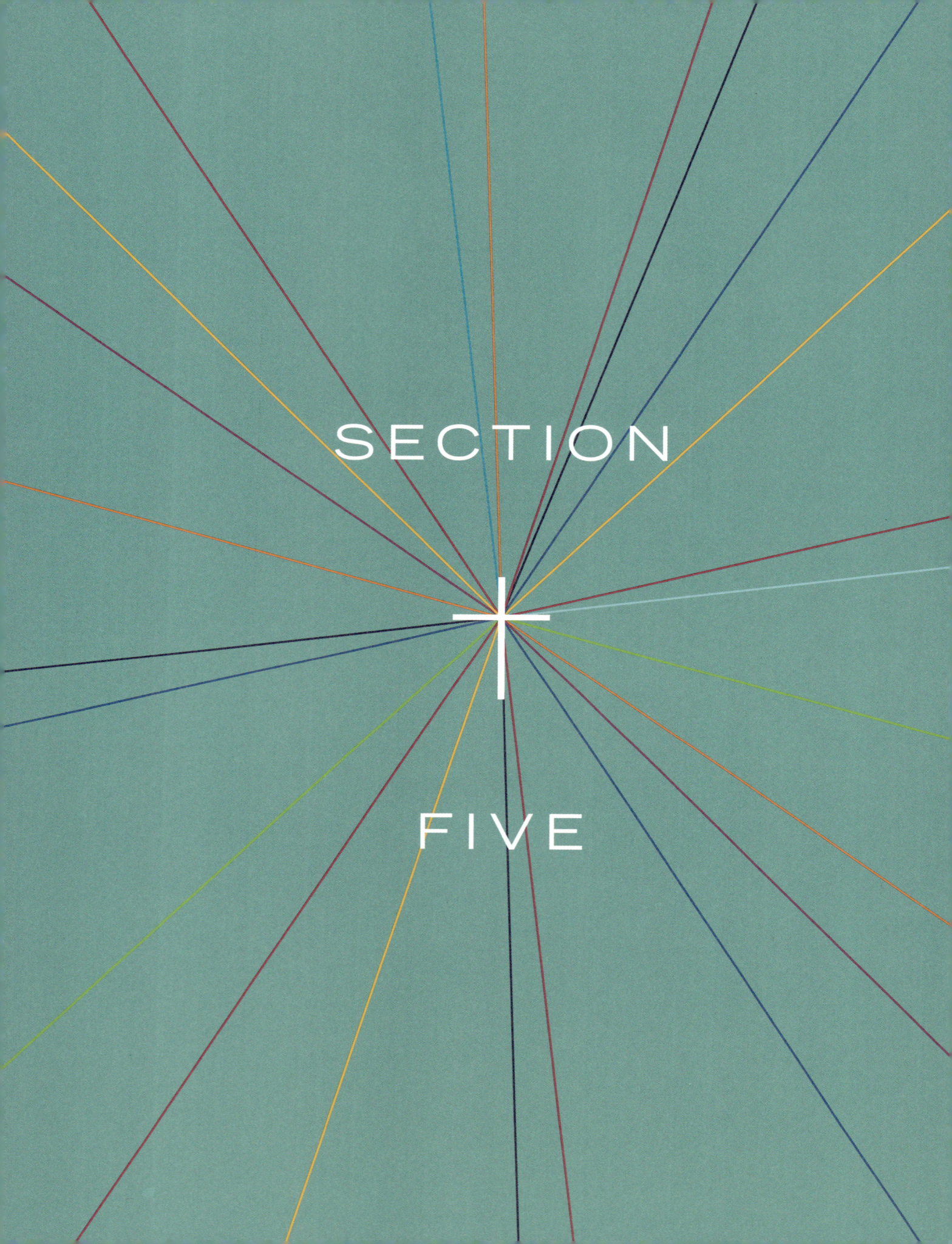

SECTION

FIVE

21

FROM SHAME TO GRACE

Key Observation
Nearly 1,500 years before Jesus, by holding up this snake on a stick, Moses was prophetically pointing toward a Messiah who would be lifted up for the sake of healing a hurting world.

Read Numbers 21:4—9.
- Explain this scene in your own words.
- What provoked God to send the snakes and how did the snakes provoke the people?
- How were people healed of their snake bites?
- How does this scene fit (or does it?) with your understanding of a good and holy God who wants the best for his people?

Spoiler alert: This story draws a straight line from Moses to the central purpose of Christ. That's why we're taking time with it now. Let's start with the fact that God knows something about snakes that the Israelites don't. With snakes, the very thing that can kill you is the thing that can make you well. In fact, in the Midwest, snakes are farmed for the specific purpose of harvesting their venom to make antivenin (the stuff that reverses the effects of a deadly snake bite). Insert that fact into the story you've just read, and now God is making a profound prophetic statement about redemption. When the whiny, contentious, rebellious, snake-bitten people of God gazed upon the bronze snake, they were reminded that sin has consequences and that only when they acknowledged their own sin would they be healed.

This points us toward the cross where we find Jesus, our sacrificial lamb, carrying our sins for us. Nearly fifteen hundred years before Jesus, by holding up this snake on a stick, Moses was prophetically pointing toward a Messiah who would be lifted up for the sake of healing a hurting world. By gazing on Christ, we find our healing. The cross is how we get from shame to grace.

Let me say that again another way: we cannot get from shame to grace without going through the cross.

> My friends, when we are redeemed, even the worst of what we have done is redeemed along with our lives.

In the transfiguration story of Luke 9, Moses, Elijah, and Jesus are brought together into one scene as a testament to the continuity of the Bible from cover to cover. The message of the whole Bible is a message of restoration. But we are forgetful people. As this story of the snakes was passed from generation to generation, its healing point got lost. The snake on a stick that used to be a testament to the miraculous power of God was reduced to mascot status, or idol status, for the Israelites. It should not surprise us to find out that eventually they named it and began to worship it. Once the point was lost, God ordered the king of Israel to smash the serpent. But Jesus, who sees the big picture, will draw on this story multiple times to help a Jewish world hear that God did not come to condemn the world but to save it. Let's keep reading.

Read John 3:14–15, then John 12:31–33.
- What connects these two passages? What is the spiritual principle at work here?

In John 3, Jesus was talking to a religious leader who had come to him at night to ask some questions. The guy was awestruck by Jesus' miracles, and he said that clearly God must be with him. Jesus responded, "Unless one is born again he cannot see the kingdom of God" (John 3:3 ESV).

This stopped the guy in his tracks. How can a full-grown man go back into his mother's womb and be born again? What Jesus wanted the man to hear is that sometimes the old has to die completely so the new can live. As part of the lesson, he drew on that old story of the snake in the desert in order to connect this man's sin to the work God was about to do in the world. He wanted this man to hear that God is not destructive but redemptive. I imagine Jesus passionately sharing this truth with the hope that the man would remember it when he saw him nailed to a cross one day. This Jesus is a sign that God did not come to condemn us but to save us. As with the snakes in the desert, the story of the cross doesn't end with death but with life. Restoration. Redemption.

FROM SHAME TO GRACE

> **Read Luke 9:30 again.**

There is Jesus with Moses and Elijah, standing on a mountain together to bear witness to the fact that God's grand redemptive plan will be carried out on earth. No amount of disobedience and no display of collective amnesia will stop God from doing what he will do. God has a plan, has had a plan from the beginning, and has not only a plan but the power to see it through.

"I, when I am lifted up from the earth, will draw all people to myself" (John 12:32). What a glorious story and what a powerful promise.

My friends, when we are redeemed, even the worst of what we have done is redeemed along with our lives. God works through the Story, and God works through our stories. He intends to use all of it for his glory! Just as the snake that was killed was lifted up and made into a sign of healing, so our stories, too, can be signs of hope and redemption for others. As with Moses and the snake, we may not understand the full impact of our stories for years but be encouraged: look to Jesus and find your healing.

Remember it is not the intention of Jesus to let you stop at the point of your own healing. "Proclaim the kingdom," he commissioned. As powerful and grace-filled as your own healing story is, it is not fully redeemed until you go back down the mountain and share the good news with others.

LISTENING TO THE WORD

Think of a story from your life that God has redeemed. Take ten minutes to write an outline of that story, then rehearse it. Ask God to give you at least one opportunity this week to share that story of God's redemptive grace and power.

22

FROM SHAME TO GRACE... TO GLORY!

Key Observation

Spiritual revelation is an invitation into the deep places where God's will is being revealed and activated.

Read Luke 9:26, then Luke 9:32.
- What is the big message of Luke 9:26 for the first-century world? What is meant by the word "ashamed"?
- Why do you suppose Jesus distinguished between himself and his words?
- Luke describes Peter and his companions as sleepy. Why? Was it because of the time of day, the pace of ministry, the intensity of following Jesus, or . . . ?
- What is the one-word connection between verse 26 and verse 32?

Beginning with Luke 9:21, Jesus was making predictions and offering up a warning or two. Having predicted his death, he gave some details about how it would happen. He showed his followers the connection between his death and the spirit of legalistic religion (a whole other sermon). He taught about the connection between our acknowledgment of God's glory and God's acknowledgment of us, warning, "Whoever is ashamed of me and my words, the Son of Man will be ashamed of them when he comes in his glory and in the glory of the Father and of the holy angels" (v. 26).

That's a hard word. Then, just after he told them some of them would see the kingdom of God, he recruited Peter, James, and John for a trip up a mountain.

FROM SHAME TO GRACE... TO GLORY!

The story goes on from there to describe what scholars call the transfiguration, a big word that means a complete change in appearance from something mortal to something divine. His three friends didn't see it coming. They were tired. When they got to the top of this hill, they were ready to rest while Jesus did whatever it is Jesus went up the hill to do.

Then—glory! Jesus was transformed into this other-world body, something seeable but hardly believable. As if that weren't enough, Moses and Elijah showed up. *The* Moses and Elijah. The disciples were slow to see it, but the story says, "When they became fully awake, they saw his glory" (Luke 9:32).

I recognize myself in the state of Jesus' disciples. What sightings of glory am I missing because I'm not fully awake? John Piper is famous for saying, "God is always doing 10,000 things in your life, and you may be aware of three of them."[10] Amen!

A couple of years ago, I was in a pretty discouraged place. We were in the middle of a building project that was stalled due to construction costs. I was slogging through a never-ending dissertation project. A denominational crisis was sucking all the joy out of life. I was just . . . *done*. I remember saying to a friend, "I'm so done with empty encouragement, from searching the Bible for some sentence that will give me hope enough to get through the day. Empty hope isn't helping. If I see one more meme with a kitten hanging onto the bottom of a rope, telling me to tie a knot and hang on, I will shoot my computer screen."

> Maybe it is time to up your prayer game. Pray your big dreams. Pray for a miracle.

I was burned out and angry with God, who seemed silent and distant. I made a decision one day and declared it to God in prayer: I would rejoice when he actually moved but I would no longer be content with vague hopes and empty encouragement. I needed to see him move.

You know what happened? God responded to my temper tantrum and started to move.

Just joking. Actually, God in his mercy gave me eyes to see what he was already up to. I realized he'd been working all around me, but I just didn't have eyes to see it. God was doing about ten thousand things, and I was only aware of three of them.

What if God is doing far more in your life and in the world around you right now, and you're just not aware of it? How can you become more aware? Let me give you three places to begin:

- **Pray that which is not as if it is.**

Often, the miracle begins when we decide to start walking in the miracle before it manifests. Let that truth impact your next prayer. Begin to pray that which is not as if it is.

- **Pray for his presence, but also pray for power.**

What if you are missing the miracles because you're spending your prayer life praying for a better parking space at Walmart? Maybe it is time to up your prayer game. Pray your big dreams. Pray for a miracle. If it doesn't happen, so be it. But what if it *does* happen?

- **Ask for eyes to see what God is already doing.**

Here is a spiritual principle worth memorizing: spiritual revelation is an invitation into the deep places where God's will is being revealed and activated. Our supernatural God is at work; our charge is to be awake to what he is doing—awakened to the glories—so we can join him in that work.

Are you open to the wonders of God?

LISTENING TO THE WORD

Paul encouraged us to go after the gift of prophecy, which is really just having eyes to see. He wrote "Follow the way of love and eagerly desire gifts of the Spirit, especially prophecy" (1 Cor. 14:1). If you have not yet desired or sought after this gift, I encourage you to do so. Spend some time in prayer, seeking the prophetic gift. Pray that God would give you eyes to see, ears to hear, and a heart to receive all he has for you and all he wants to do *through* you. Pray specifically for an understanding of the prophetic gift and how it might play out in your life.

23

CLOUD, FIRE, AND GLORY

Key Observation
"If you love the way God shows up, it is a good sign that you want more of God; if you love what God chooses to do, it is a good sign that you want more of God." — R. T. Kendall

> **Read Exodus 40:34–38, then read Acts 1:8 and Acts 2:1–4.**
> - What is the relationship between the cloud and God's glory in the Exodus passage?
> - What do you learn about glory from the scene in Exodus?
> - What connection do you see between these three passages?

This scene from Exodus is our backdrop for Pentecost. The Israelites had just finished the building of the tabernacle, which would accompany them through their remaining desert travels and into the land promised by God. When the tabernacle was completed, God inhabited it with signs of cloud, fire, and glory. And the instructions were clear: when God moves, the people move.

The tabernacle of the Old Testament became the church in the New Testament. In the beginning of the book of Acts, the resurrected Jesus was telling his followers, "You will receive power when the Holy Spirit comes on you; and you will be my witnesses in Jerusalem, and in all Judea and Samaria, and to the ends of the earth" (1:8). When New Testament followers of Jesus were given the charge to follow the Holy Spirit out into the world, they became the new tabernacle of God. Like the Israelites in the desert, they received both fire and a pervading presence of God's Spirit as signs of his presence and power.

Acts 1:8 promises power. "You *will* receive power when the Holy Spirit comes on you." Not "you *might* receive," or "if you're lucky you'll receive." Nope. Jesus said, "You *will* receive power"—the same power the Israelites had, the Israelites who fought with enemies twice their size and won, who found enough food to feed hundreds of thousands of people, who received miracle after miracle of God's provision. That same power would send Jesus' followers out into surrounding villages to cast out demons, cure diseases, proclaim the kingdom, and heal the sick. And that same power would propel disciples out into the world to speak the gospel in many languages so that in one day three thousand people would be saved.

The power they had we now have. When we are filled with the Holy Spirit, when we receive that kind of power and take authority over it to cast out demons, cure diseases, heal the sick, and proclaim the kingdom, we become the answer to Jesus' own prayer: "Your kingdom come, your will be done, on earth [right here . . . right now] as it is in heaven" (Matt. 6:10).

> **Read Luke 9:33–35 and Matthew 17:1–9.**
> - Compare these two versions of this story. What are the distinctives between them?
> - What is the effect of the cloud on the witnesses? What is the effect of the voice they hear?

All the above teaching from Exodus and Acts sets us up for what happened in Luke 9. Just as in Exodus 40 and Acts 1, a cloud appeared and a voice affirmed the power of God in the transfiguration story. It must have been stunning and mind-blowing to be present on the mountain that day. Peter was so awestruck by the whole scene that he wanted to stay in it. "Let's stay here!" he said. As if they could chuck the rest of the mission and camp out. But Jesus would have none of that. He sent them back down to the valley and into the work for which they had been equipped. That display of power they had seen was not for them only but for them to share. We experience the glory of God on our way to proclaiming the in-breaking kingdom!

> **When we are filled with the Holy Spirit, we become the answer to Jesus' own prayer: "Your kingdom come, your will be done, on earth [right here . . . right now] as it is in heaven" (Matt. 6:10).**

In a *Charisma Magazine* article, R. T. Kendall remembered Jack Hayford's experience of seeing the glory of God manifest in his church. I have heard Dr. Hayford tell the story firsthand, but I like the way Kendall relates the glory sighting to kingdom fruit:

CLOUD, FIRE, AND GLORY

I once heard Pastor Jack Hayford tell of an event that took place in his church years ago on a Saturday. He looked inside the auditorium and saw a haze.

"It's what you think it is," the Lord said to him.

This happened when his church was young, with an attendance of perhaps three hundred. After that day his church began to grow and grow until it reached thousands. Jack traces this growth to that Saturday when he saw the haze.

Do you want more of God? If so, you must love the glory of God, which means you must appreciate the way he chooses to show up—however uncomfortable it makes you feel—but also accept his will—no matter how disappointed you may be.

Jonathan Edwards taught that the one thing Satan cannot do is give one a love for God's glory. If you love the way God shows up, it is a good sign that you want more of God; if you love what God chooses to do, it is a good sign that you want more of God.[11]

Without the mountaintop experiences, we burn out. Without the valley, we bear no fruit. The time on the mountain informs time in the valley. Without the mountain, the valley is just us collecting merit badges for doing good things.

Mountain and valley, cloud and fire. This is the rhythm of the supernatural life.

LISTENING TO THE WORD

> Kendall wrote, "Jonathan Edwards taught that the one thing Satan cannot do is give one a love for God's glory. If you love the way God shows up, it is a good sign that you want more of God." Do you want more of God? What choices do you need to make so there is both daily and weekly space for seeking after the presence, power, and glory of God?

24

TALKING ABOUT GLORY

Key Observation
I believe our energy and interest ought always to be weighted more toward redemption and exposing the kingdom of God than on miracles and manifestations.

Read Luke 9:36, and then read Mark 1:40–45.
- What do you notice about both of these passages?
- In the Luke account, what about this incident caused the disciples not to tell anyone?
- In the Mark story, Jesus asked the man not to tell anyone about his miracle. Why?
- Can you imagine seeing or experiencing something as powerful and otherworldly as a glory sighting or miracle, and not telling anyone about it? What might prompt you to stay quiet?

I'm guessing we can all agree on this point: our world has far too many negative vibes and far too little good news (thank you, social media). In a world with too much negativity, our attitude toward good news is that it ought to be shared. Our assumption is that good news will affect others for the better and will adjust attitudes and give hope.

Why, then, might Jesus have asked folks not to talk about the miracles he had done among them? The story in Mark 1 (one of several where Jesus asks someone not to share their experience) gives us a clue. Mark recorded the man who had received the miracle immediately was excited over being healed, so he went out and began to talk freely about it. "As a result, Jesus could no longer

TALKING ABOUT GLORY

enter a town openly but stayed outside in lonely places. Yet the people still came to him from everywhere" (Mark 1:45).

The work wasn't destroyed by the man's rebellious insistence on telling his story, but it did create challenges both for Jesus and those whom he could heal. One reason Jesus told people to keep these healing stories to themselves was that he had a big-picture view of the plan of God that others did not have.

It is also possible that the man's news would have traveled to the temple faster than the man could. He had been healed of leprosy and was told by Jesus to present himself to the priest and offer sacrifices so he could be completely restored into the community. But if he didn't go at once—if he delayed while telling his story to everyone in his own circle—opponents of Jesus' ministry might have gone on ahead of him and prejudiced the priest's opinions about the guy. Talk might have cast a shadow of a doubt over this miracle.

That shouldn't surprise us. How often do we respond skeptically to news about megapastors and megachurches doing great things? How many of us have shaken our heads at stories online that seem too supernatural to be true? And, yes, some of them *are* too good to be true (or too fake to be true). But not all are this way. I once heard a well-respected man of God admire the work of someone who most of America made fun of. He said, "He is so misunderstood. He is actually a gentle, faithful man who is trying to live out his call and who has a miraculous healing ministry that has touched thousands of lives." I have been humbled by that comment and wonder how often I've tossed skepticism in the face of authentic supernatural ministry giftings.

No wonder not all stories ought to be shared! Sometimes hiddenness in ministry is not a matter of ineffectiveness or even false humility but a matter of being as wise as a serpent—of giving God the most room to work. I wonder, too, if Jesus recognized that some of those he healed were more interested in the miracle than the man— that when they went out to talk about what they'd seen, they'd talk more like folks who had won a prize at the fair than as folks who had brushed up against heaven itself. When a person is ignorant or unfaithful, their comments about Christ can actually do more harm than good. There is a lot to be said for knowing what you're talking about before you open your mouth.

> What choice, concern, or vision in your life needs less conversation and more percolation through the Holy Spirit?

And, interestingly, people who know what they are talking about often say less than those who don't. Curious, that.

SUPERNATURAL

As I write this, it is just a few days before Christmas, so my mind is on the manger. I'm thinking about Mary's visitation by an angel and about how she heard and saw things that would blow my mind. Being an external processor, I would have been telling everyone and their sister all I'd seen. Mary, by contrast, seems to have chosen the better option. She visited with her relative, Elizabeth, where she got prophetic wisdom. Then she began to walk out her own miracle and "treasured up all these things and pondered them in her heart" (Luke 2:19).

That's wisdom. To allow the big things to percolate in our spirits, to seek out prophetic wisdom (not just good advice, but spiritual insight), and to trust God with our reputation is surely the better path. Sometimes the most effective way we can participate in the supernatural is to sit still, listen for the voice of God, and practice restraint until he sends us out.

I believe our energy and interest ought always to be weighted toward redemption and exposing the kingdom of God than on miracles and manifestations. Those things matter and are great gifts to the body of Christ, but they are not the goal. They are tools in the service of the goal, which is always to expose the kingdom of God.

LISTENING TO THE WORD

What choice, concern, or vision in your life needs less conversation and more percolation through the Holy Spirit? What vision actually needs to be incubated before you share it at all? Spend time journaling about that issue now, and make a fresh commitment to seeking first the kingdom of God.

25

A RELIGION OF MIRACLES

Key Observation
Every miracle in the Bible exposed the kingdom of God and fulfilled Isaiah's prophecy that the Messiah would bind up the broken-hearted, set captives free, give sight to the blind, and release those imprisoned by demons.

Read Luke 9:6 and Luke 9:27.
- What is the relationship between the four action verbs in these verses in Luke 9?
- Given what you've learned so far, what do you think it looks like to see the kingdom of God exposed on earth?

Thomas Jefferson once took a pen knife and cut most of the miracle stories out of the Bible, leaving only the teachings of Jesus. He left the tomb but cut out the resurrection. What was left, which was mostly the teachings of Jesus, Jefferson entitled, "The Philosophy of Jesus of Nazareth."

What Jefferson did to the Bible with a pen knife, many contemporary Christians unwittingly do with their lives. Especially in the United States, much of Christian culture has managed to surgically remove the supernatural from the experience of Jesus of Nazareth. We've fallen out of the habit of talking publicly and passionately about how to transform lives. We will talk about decline in church attendance, the cultural shift away from Christendom, and the declining morals of our society, but we have neither the vocabulary nor the comfort for talking about the spiritual realm. Yet, according to Jesus himself, the work of God is to see the kingdom break in through the supernatural work of casting

SUPERNATURAL

out demons, curing diseases, healing the sick, and seeing people transformed by truth (Luke 9:1–2).

Christianity is not a faith with a few miracles sprinkled in for effect. Christianity is a *miracle* with some good stories thrown in. Miracles are the cornerstone of the Christian faith. To extract them from the gospel of Jesus Christ would be to extract the heart of God for the people he created.

Without miracles, we lose the divinity of Jesus. Without the virgin birth, Jesus is just another kid born to an unwed mother. He begins to look more like Buddha or Mohammed and less like a God in the flesh. We believe Jesus is worthy of worship, but he is only worthy if he has been proven to be God himself.

Without miracles, we lose hope. We have no assurance of an afterlife if Jesus didn't supernaturally conquer death, nor any reason to assume that the cross has power to cancel sin.

> Christianity is the ongoing presence and power of the Holy Spirit transforming the natural through the invasion of the supernatural.

Without miracles, we lose touch with the essential character of God. Psalm 145 tells us that we are to pass the stories of God's mighty acts from generation to generation, because it is the mighty acts of God—not morality—that teach us about God's character and purposes. Through his miracles (the parting of the Red Sea, the miraculous catch of fish, the woman whose oil lasted through a famine, the drowning of a legion of demons), we see God's goodness and that he is for us.

Without miracles, we have no insight into the kingdom of God. The point of miracles is to draw us into the realm of God's kingdom and influence. All over the world right now, stories are surfacing of Muslims, Buddhists, and Hindus being drawn into the kingdom through miracles and visions. They are being introduced to Jesus by Jesus himself in supernatural encounters. Why? Because Jesus wants to see these cultures restored to the kingdom of God.

Every miracle in the Bible exposed the kingdom of God and fulfilled Isaiah's prophecy that the Messiah would bind up the brokenhearted, set captives free, give sight to the blind, and release those imprisoned by demons. This was a foretaste of coming attractions, of Jesus demonstrating kingdom values.

With all due respect to President Jefferson, Christianity is not a philosophy. It is a declaration of the one true God—the most powerful Being in the universe—and his supernatural revelation through Jesus Christ. Christianity is the ongoing

A RELIGION OF MIRACLES

presence and power of the Holy Spirit transforming the natural through the invasion of the supernatural. If we want to see the kingdom come, it will happen as we openly, boldly acknowledge that Jesus was and is not just a great cultural stabilizer but a supernatural God whose resurrection leads those who follow him directly into the supernatural realm.

Richard Rohr, Catholic priest and spiritual director, wrote,

> *As priests, we felt our job was to absolve sin, rather than actually transform people. "Get rid of the contaminating element," as it were, rather than, "Learn what you can about yourself and God because of this conflict." Those are two very different paths.... In the four Gospels Jesus did two things over and over again:* he preached and he healed. *We do a lot of preaching, but not too much healing.*[12]

In Richard Rohr's confession, he went on from the above quote to diagnose the why behind his assertion. He said that we've done more preaching than healing, not because our hearts are hard (though undoubtedly that's true for some) or because we don't find it important, but because we don't know how. We have forgotten, if we ever knew, how to call the people in our care into deeper spiritual waters.

Without miracles, we are not pursuing the whole gospel, the deeper waters of our faith. In Luke 9:6, we are told that the disciples went from village to village, preaching and healing. The message traveled via the miracles. In other words, heal the sick and proclaim the kingdom, cast out demons and proclaim the kingdom, cure diseases and proclaim the kingdom. If you don't do the second part, the first part doesn't matter. But the first part is what separates us from nothing more than a good story and some moral platitudes.

LISTENING TO THE WORD

Pick someone. Go ahead. Pick someone who needs healing, and start praying for that person today. After a few days, go find that person and say you've been praying for him or her. Then tell about the hope you have within you that causes you to have faith enough to pray . . . both for his or her healing and yours.

Group Gathering

OPEN WITH PRAYER

WATCH SESSION 5 VIDEO

DISCUSS THE FOLLOWING QUESTIONS BASED ON READINGS 21–25

21

Key Observation
Nearly 1,500 years before Jesus, by holding up this snake on a stick, Moses was prophetically pointing toward a Messiah who would be lifted up for the sake of healing a hurting world.

Question for Discussion
How does it encourage your faith to see how Old and New Testament stories weave together to form one unbroken message of redemption?

22

Key Observation
Spiritual revelation is an invitation into the deep places where God's will is being revealed and activated.

Question for Discussion
How familiar are you with the concept of spiritual revelation? How does God most often reveal himself and his truths to you?

23

Key Observation
"If you love the way God shows up, it is a good sign that you want more of God; if you love what God chooses to do, it is a good sign that you want more of God." — R. T. Kendall

Question for Discussion
Has this study caused you to question what you know about how God shows up? In what ways?

24

Key Observation
I believe our energy and interest ought always to be weighted more toward redemption and exposing the kingdom of God than on miracles and manifestations.

Question for Discussion
If miracles and manifestations still matter, then what does this statement teach you about what ought to motivate us in our pursuit of them?

25

Key Observation
Every miracle in the Bible exposed the kingdom of God and fulfilled Isaiah's prophecy that the Messiah would bind up the broken-hearted, set captives free, give sight to the blind, and release those imprisoned by demons.

Question for Discussion
What does this teach you about prophecy? About the values of the kingdom of God?

CLOSE WITH PRAYER

Prophetic intercession is a way of praying that calls that which is not as if it is (see Hebrews 11:1). As the group closes in prayer, spend time calling out in prayer those things we believe to be true, though they have not yet manifested. Pray prophetically over someone who is addicted as if they can be sober. Pray against someone who is sick as if they can be healed. Pray those things on earth that we know to be true about heaven, where there is no war, no racism, no pain, no killing; and where there is forgiveness and peace and wholeness.

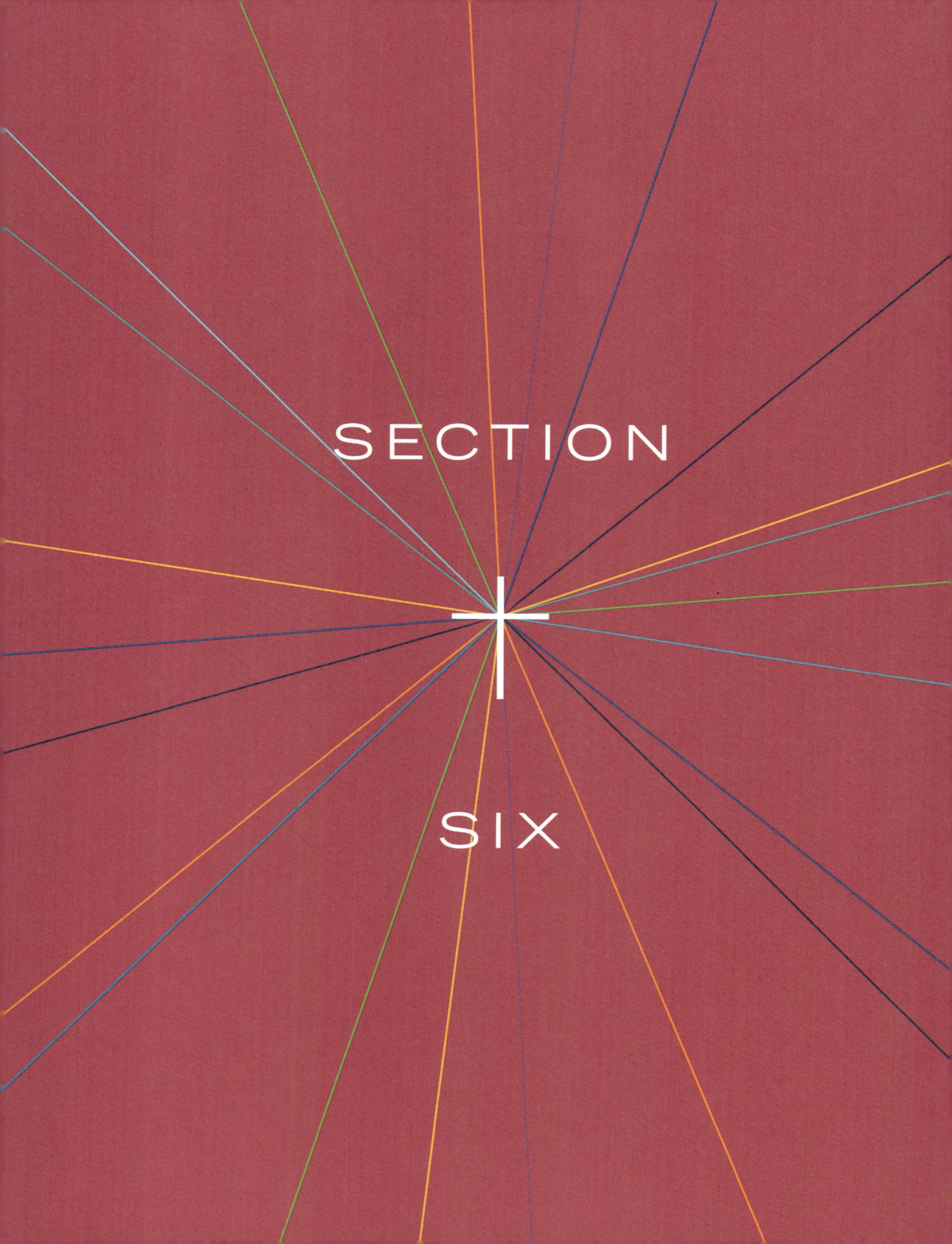

SECTION

SIX

WHAT WE KNOW ABOUT THE ENEMY OF OUR SOULS

Key Observation

Knowing the Enemy seems important if we are going to use the power and authority given us to defeat him.

Read Luke 9:37–42.

- What does this story teach you about the authority of Christ?
- What do you learn about spiritual warfare just from this story? What do you believe? What are your questions?

In the commissioning recorded in Luke 9, Jesus asked his followers to do what he had just modeled for them in Luke 8. He asked them to go out into surrounding towns and villages, giving them power and authority to cast out demons, cure diseases, proclaim the kingdom, and heal the sick. And this is exactly what they did.

Fast-forward to the middle of Luke 9, and we find the followers of Jesus frustrated over a stubborn demon who wouldn't leave a little boy. With stories like this one, it is easy to turn them into metaphors—making the demon into something less than a real spiritual force and making the boy's suffering into the effects of his own wrestling. Too quickly, we could make this story about our own issues, which may not *fall* into the category of uncontrolled demon possession.

SUPERNATURAL

Here's what we know. This boy was suffering. He couldn't have understood what was happening. His father was on the deep end of desperation, as we would be too. Can you imagine these symptoms in your child? Can you imagine watching as your son was thrown around by something you couldn't define, control, or fix?

When Jesus stepped into this situation, he seemed more put off by the people in the story than by the demons. He seemed bothered by disciples who—given power and authority (see Luke 9:1–2)—can't seem to cast out a simple demon from a little boy. This teaches us something about Jesus. Remember, Jesus took demons seriously, but he never allowed them to control him.

> **The Enemy's first language is lies. The best he can do is attach his message to a feeling. He does not operate in the realm of facts.**

This story also teaches us something about the effect demons have on people. The boy was controlled. The father was desperate. The disciples were powerless. The people were in awe. But Jesus, who surely had eyes to see what was happening on the spiritual plane, was merely annoyed! From the context, it seems to me that the more you know about demons, the less threatening they are.

Sun Tzu, in a book called *The Art of War*, wrote, "If you know the enemy and know yourself, you need not fear the result of a hundred battles. If you know yourself but not the enemy, for every victory gained you will also suffer a defeat. If you know neither the enemy nor yourself, you will succumb in every battle."[13]

Knowing the Enemy seems important if we are going to use the power and authority given us to defeat him. What do you know about the Enemy of your soul? Here are some things I've learned about spiritual warfare, evil, and the Enemy of our souls:

✷ **Evil spirits exist.** It would be very difficult to trust the Bible if we didn't believe this. So much of the story of God is predicated on the battle between God's armies of angels and Satan's army of demons. Jesus engaged demons on multiple occasions. He spoke directly to them, proving they are personal beings with the capacity to communicate.

✷ **Demons can enter people and control them.** We learn this from this story because the boy was possessed by a demon. We also know that demons can pester people without possessing them (see Zechariah 3:1–2 for an excellent example of this). My personal belief is that we are a one-car garage. Once we have invited Jesus into our lives, he will prevent Satan from occupying the same space. That does not mean, however, that the Enemy won't continue to pester us from the outside. He is a

WHAT WE KNOW ABOUT THE ENEMY OF OUR SOULS

whisperer. He loves to whisper hints into unstable moments to tempt us into sin. He is good at breeding discouragement. This is the bigger problem for most of us—not that we'll be possessed, but that we'll be pestered.

* **Jesus didn't play games with demons.** He clearly had power over them, but he didn't take them lightly. The story in Luke 9 is a clear example of how annoying he found them to be and how much he wanted his own followers to own their power over the Enemy.

* **The Enemy is lazy.** He will default to the path of least resistance every time. He looks for our weaknesses so he can exploit them. He loves to divide people, groups, and even create division within each of us. This is why daily discipline is so crucial. It arms us against the Enemy's worst.

* **The Enemy's first language is lies.** Let that sink in. Nothing we hear from Satan is true. Nothing. Even his confessions of Christ or his quoting of Scripture are hollow, because while he knows truth he can't accept it. The best he can do is attach his message to a feeling. He does not operate in the realm of facts. Knowing this helps us interpret temptations, deception, and discouragement. If the thing we are hearing is all feeling, not fact, then we know it is a lie of the Enemy.

* **We know how the story ends, and the Enemy doesn't win.** He can destroy in the short-term but not in the long-term. Your eternal security is safely kept by grace through faith in the One who wins.

LISTENING TO THE WORD

List the places in your life where you'd say you are most vulnerable. Then list the ways the Enemy tends to capitalize on those weaknesses. Finally, list the ways you can combat those attacks—make sure you include prayer in that list. Conclude this time in prayer, asking Christ Jesus to strengthen you against your Enemy (and his).

27

JESUS WINS

Key Observation
I believe our sent-ness is to the same things that called the Israelites out of Egypt. It is a call to choose life and reject the powers of hell and death.

Read Luke 9:49–50.
- How did the guy who was casting out demons in Jesus' name know the name of Jesus was powerful enough to overpower demons?
- How is supernatural ministry connected to the process or journey of sanctification?

In Luke 9 we get not one but two stories dealing with demons. That's worth noticing because Luke 9 does not include two healing stories or two salvation stories, but there are two stories about casting out demons. In the scene in verses 49–50, a guy was casting out demons, and Jesus' followers didn't know him and asked him to stop. Then in the next scene, when they got a little pushback from the religious leaders in Jerusalem, they had the nerve to actually ask Jesus if they can rain fire down on a few heads. By Jesus' response to both these actions, we get the sense that the disciples have issues with fear and defensiveness.

Meanwhile, when Jesus talked about casting out demons, it sounded like the most normal thing in the world. "Hey, y'all! Let's head on over to the local coffee shop and cast out some demons!" For Jesus, this is life. Life contains friction. How we deal with it makes all the difference in the world. I believe Jesus wants us to embrace the power he gives us over spiritual darkness. I absolutely believe we are called to be in a partnership with him against the forces of evil.

JESUS WINS

My ministry is mostly experimental. Inner healing has been a place where I've seen the most fruit. I've prayed for people to be physically healed and have seen some results. These days, what most excites me is how a willingness to experiment is rubbing off on the next generation. This year, a student in our community went on a mission trip with her classmates. Early on during the trip, she had a dream that turned out to be prophetic. I'll let her tell the story:

I had a prophetic dream. The team going to the Bahamas was standing before a village at night and all the lights were out, and I could feel the presence of evil in it. Then Jesus filled us all up with authority, and we began to march around the streets of the village, casting evil out in the name of Jesus, and every time we would do so, a light would turn on in the houses around us. We kept doing so until the entire village was blazing with light, and the power of the Holy Spirit flooded the streets. Waking up from that I knew God had something great in mind.

(Later) I was with our group and we prayed over people . . . then my friend pulled me aside and told me, "I remember you telling us last night about how God has given us the power to cast out demons. There is a man over there who we believe has an evil spirit. Do you want to come and pray over him?"[14]

Our student and several others did pray over this person. Over the next several days, they continued to pray, each time sensing that God was doing something in his life. Each time, he was less resistant to their prayers than the time before, and each time they shared with him the love of Jesus and their own love for him. On the last day of the trip, they found the man in the village and prayed over him one last time. It was then that the student sensed the Enemy had released his grip on this man.

He just began saying, "Thank you, God. Thank you, God. Thank you, God." And hearing these words from his mouth, I knew victory had come. . . . Nothing crazy happened when he was released from the spirit of confinement, but you could tell in his countenance that something had changed. The Enemy works in different ways, and it is important to be aware at all times so you can be ready when an opportunity presents itself. Don't be afraid. Know that God will always be victorious.[15]

> Jesus wants us to embrace the power he gives us over spiritual darkness.

And that is the advice of a pretty amazing sixteen-year-old high school student who loves Jesus and has decided to take him at his word.

Do I believe we have power and authority to cast out demons? Yes, I do. And I also believe the Lord longs to see his church acting as if he is a supernatural

SUPERNATURAL

God and supernatural power is ours. I believe our sent-ness is to the same things that called the Israelites out of Egypt. It is a call to choose life and reject the powers of hell and death.

We serve an apartment complex in downtown Augusta for low- and no-income adults with disabilities. We go with food and prayer, and we get lengthy lists of prayer requests. I was praying through that list one day: *Jan needs help finding dental insurance to get dentures. Jamelia wants complete healing from her recent stroke. Dixie doesn't want to be alone for the holidays.* And then buried in this long list was this request: *Roger asks that Satan would soon be thrown into the fiery pit.*

I pumped my fist in the air when I read that prayer request and prayed in agreement with Roger. *Yes, Roger, yes!* And based on Luke 9, it looks like we have permission to pray that prayer with confidence and to trust that through our prayers and our Spirit-desperate ministry God intends to do just that. So hang on, Roger, because Jesus wins.

LISTENING TO THE WORD

What do you hope to see in your church as you (and others) embrace supernatural healing and deliverance as a normal practice of the Christian life? Make this a prayer, asking God to make you bolder for the sake of the gospel.

28

THE KINGDOM ADVANCES

Key Observation
The kingdom suffers the violence of a demonic world that has lost the war but continues to fight battles on its way to final, full defeat.

Read Luke 11:14—28.

- (Yes, I know I'm cheating a little here. We've jumped ship on Luke 9, but only so we can dig deeper into what Jesus knew to be true about the demonic realm. Go with me on this, and I promise you'll see something new.)
- If you had to boil the theme of this passage down to one sentence, what would it be? What is the overall message?
- What strikes you about how Jesus handled both his detractors and his supporters? How would you characterize his responses to each?
- Count the number of times the word "kingdom" is used in this passage. What do you learn from this passage about the kingdom of God?

Jesus clearly had power over demons. He approached them seriously but not fearfully. He seemed to understand how the mere presence of demons creates confusion. This is a spiritual principle worth remembering: demons create confusion. Since they don't deal in the whole truth, they tend to bring fear, anxiety, and confusion into any situation they enter. If you're in a situation that seems to get more tangled and confused as it goes, suspect it. Chances are, the Enemy is not far away.

Take the example of the story we've just read. Jesus cast out a demon, and immediately those who didn't understand such things began to generate rumors and falsehoods. "If he can talk to demons, then maybe he is one!" Jesus responded by teaching them how things work in the kingdom of God. This was in keeping with Jesus' overarching mission. Jesus never moved far from the topic of the kingdom of God. He was always trying to get us to see it, grasp it, and embrace it. It is like a seed, like soil, like leaven, like something valuable buried in a field. Something ordinary, sometimes hidden, that possesses an unexpected strength.

That unexpected strength is constantly in tension with the anti-kingdom. This, we have already said, is where Luke 9 intersects with the holiness code of Leviticus. After the Israelites were set free from slavery in Egypt, the Lord established a code of life among them that reflected his holy design. That code required that they constantly root out and destroy signs of Egypt, signs of death, and signs of the anti-kingdom. Luke 9 takes up that same task as Jesus sent his followers out with power and authority to cast out demons, cure diseases, proclaim the kingdom, and heal the sick. He says, in effect, "Wherever you see them—demons, disease, sickness—you cast out death and proclaim life over my people."

> The Enemy has lost the war, and if we will take authority as Jesus has given us permission to do, then the Enemy will also lose the battles he wages in your life and mine.

All this is to say that the kingdom of God is constantly at war with the kingdom of darkness. In the book of Matthew, Jesus used a word that reveals this characteristic of the kingdom. He said, "From the days of John the Baptist until now the kingdom of heaven has suffered violence, and the violent take it by force" (Matt. 11:12 ESV). Another version phrases it this way: "The Kingdom of Heaven has been forcefully advancing, and violent people are attacking it" (NLT).

The Greek word used here is *biazetai*. Depending on how you use it in a sentence, it can have either of the meanings previously noted ("suffered violence" or "forcefully advancing"), though they are markedly different.

So which is it?

Is the kingdom of God suffering passively, enduring the violence of a nonbelieving world and overactive demons until the day when it finally conquers? Or is the kingdom of God actively, forcefully pushing through, refusing to take no for an answer and refusing to be laid aside by people who are surprised by the way it looks?

So is the kingdom of God suffering violence or forcefully advancing? Some years ago, I heard Timothy Tennent, president of Asbury Theological Seminary, preach on this verse and his remarks have stayed with me. Tennent said the answer to this question is yes. The kingdom of heaven suffers

THE KINGDOM ADVANCES

the violence of people who don't get who Jesus really is. The kingdom suffers the violence of laziness, the violence of unbelief, of hard hearts and broken hearts. The kingdom suffers the violence of the dark, of a kind of deafness to the sound of holiness. And the kingdom suffers the violence of a demonic world that has lost the war but continues to fight battles on its way to final, full defeat.

Yet *the kingdom never quits coming.* It never gives up, never gives in, never lets go, and never loses sight of the work.

Jesus himself said that when he is casting out demons by the power of God, then the kingdom of God has arrived (Luke 11:20)! Which means that when I see a demon leave someone's being, I'm actually seeing the kingdom of God manifested on earth. When a demon is defeated through the power of prayer, we are experiencing the advancing kingdom. The kingdom of God is as close as our next victory over the darkness. This is huge! We can experience the coming kingdom!

Be encouraged, dear friends. The Enemy has lost the war, and if we will take authority as Jesus has given us permission to do, then the Enemy will also lose the battles he wages in your life and mine. In the bargain, we will begin to expose the kingdom of God, revealing God's power on earth.

LISTENING TO THE WORD

> Take time to consider where you are in the mix of spiritual things and how connected you are to the cause of the kingdom. Are you bumping up against the powers and principalities of the dark world? Are there areas of darkness you can begin to take authority over in prayer? Make a prayer that reflects what is being revealed to you right now.

29

THE FINGER OF GOD

Key Observation
This is our trust. We have been entrusted with both the gospel and its expansion on earth. Spreading it means taking risks, crossing into enemy territory, being bold and courageous.

Read Luke 11:17–22.

- Using only this passage, make notes about everything it teaches you about Satan, about the kingdom of God, and about the struggle between them.
- Jesus uses two names for Satan in this passage—Satan and Beelzebul. Using a Bible dictionary (or Google), look up the word Beelzebul. What do you learn?

There is an interesting phrase in this passage: "the finger of God" (v. 20). What is accomplished with the finger of God? Why do you suppose it is worded this way? That phrase is found in two other places in the Bible (Ex. 8:17–19; 31:18). Read these references and compare them. How is the finger of God used in each of these instances?

I can't help but notice that in Luke 11:21, the verse that follows the "the finger of God" phrase, Jesus described the Enemy as "a strong man, fully armed" guarding his own house. Jesus went on to say, "But when someone stronger attacks and overpowers him, he takes away the armor in which the man trusted" (v. 22). On one hand (pun intended), we have a finger. On the other hand, we have a fully armed strong man. According to Jesus, the finger wins! That ought to tell us something about the difference between the power of God and the power of our Enemy.

THE FINGER OF GOD

It reminds me of how my daughter experienced my presence on a playground when she was little. Often, when I would pick her up after school, she'd be happily playing with friends on the playground and not ready to go home. When I walked onto the playground, she'd ignore me to buy time. I'd call out, but she'd deflect. Eventually, when she didn't come to my calls, I'd hold up one index finger. Claire Marie knew what it meant. It meant I was a third of the way to three fingers, and three fingers as far as she was concerned was Armageddon. Never mind that she never once let me get all three fingers in the air. Never once did she experience whatever wrath she imagined would be unleashed when I reached three fingers. Just that one finger was enough to snap her into high gear. She would be by my side, smiling up at me with that bribery smile, like all she wanted in the world was to leave with me.

> We have been entrusted with both the gospel and its expansion on earth. Spreading it means taking risks, crossing into enemy territory, and being bold and courageous.

One finger had that kind of power. I suspect I'm not alone in that way. I suspect most moms have some kind of sign language in their arsenal that wields that kind of power. So when I see "the finger of God" in Scripture and read about its power to hand down laws and induce plagues and stop the Enemy in his tracks, that's what I think of. I think of a one-finger motion that carries incredible influence. God has more power in one finger, in one gesture, than Satan has on his best day with all his armor on. Keep that in mind when you're quaking in fear or when you're assigning every wrong move or motive in your life to the Enemy of your soul. He only has the power you give him.

As John has so wisely written, "the one who is in you is greater than the one who is in the world" (1 John 4:4). Never forget that.

Read Luke 11:23.
- To what do you think Jesus was referring to when he talked about gathering?
- What does this teach you about what it means to be "with" Jesus? Is it a matter of belief or a matter of action, according to this passage?

Compare Luke 9:50 with Luke 11:23.
- What is the context of each verse? Are they saying the same thing?

These verses give us a clear choice. In Luke 11:23, Jesus said, "Whoever is not with me is against me, and whoever does not gather with me scatters." We find this line right in the middle of a conversation about spiritual warfare, so it is pretty clear what is being communicated here. Pick your side, Jesus said. When he said, "Whoever does not gather with me scatters," he's talking about gathering as a spiritual work and as a participation in the spiritual battle. Gathering is an active involvement in the process, not a sideline activity.

Meanwhile, when Jesus says in Luke 9:50, "Whoever is not against you is for you," he is inviting his followers into risk-taking ministry. Here's what I believe about the call on those who follow Jesus. I believe we are called to take some risks. We push back against the darkness, knowing we have the power of God behind us, the finger of God poised and pointed toward the Enemy. We fight because we've been given the commission to cast out demons as we proclaim the kingdom of God. We fight for the souls of people and the values of Jesus.

Paul wrote, "Now it is required that those who have been given a trust must prove faithful" (1 Cor. 4:2). This is our trust. We have been entrusted with *both the gospel and its expansion on earth*. Spreading it means taking risks, crossing into enemy territory, and being bold and courageous. This kingdom-advancing, kingdom-exposing work is the work of a warrior. It does not mean pulling up a chair and watching the battle but requires getting in there to fight it. Clearly, if we are not fighting the battle, the Enemy is gaining territory.

So fight, people. Fight for the gospel. Don't sit passively by and hope for the best or assume it will happen without you. You've been given a trust, and Christ is counting on you. Where are you invested?

LISTENING TO THE WORD

Reflect for a moment on two words found in Luke 11:23: *gathering* and *scattering*. By kingdom standards, where in your life are you gathering? Where are you scattering, perhaps unwittingly? Where are you investing time and energy?

30

EXPOSING THE KINGDOM OF GOD

Key Observation
What is the mission of God's people? To connect with the heart of God, to share God's work of salvation and revelation, and to expose the kingdom of God and the cosmic reign of Jesus Christ over all things. In short, we exist to welcome and advance the kingdom of God.

> **Read Luke 4:1–13, 31–37, 40–41; 8:1–2, 26–39; 9:37–43; 10:17–20; 22:31.**
> - What patterns do you see at work in each of these settings?
> - How is the deliverance from demonic possession usually accomplished? By touching, praying, or proclamation?
> - If you had to sum up Jesus' approach to the demonic world in one word or phrase (using the passages to inform your answer), what would it be?
> - How does this study affect your thoughts on the call to cast out demons? Are you inspired, empowered, and energized? Or wary and warned?

The Bible teaches that at Pentecost the Holy Spirit was poured out on all believers—and is still being poured out, giving all of us power and authority to cast out demons, cure diseases, proclaim the kingdom, and heal the sick. Our part is to take authority and begin to practice that power.

The key is not the type of work or the outcome. The key is how our hearts connect with the heart of God. What is the mission of God's people? To connect with the heart of God, to share God's work of salvation and revelation, and to expose the kingdom of God and the cosmic reign of Jesus Christ over all things. It is his rule that will ultimately destroy the destroyer. But we are powerful partners in that work because we are sent by God himself and by the authority of his Word. Those who follow Jesus are salt and light, fully devoted, no matter how intense the battle is. We see the world from the kingdom down rather than the world up. We understand that spiritual warfare is a normal part of a follower's life.

The end of all our work is to bring others into the throne room where they can freely and joyfully worship the living God. This is the work of the church, and this is what makes us different from all other people on earth. We exist to welcome and advance the kingdom of God.

With that motive in mind, let's discuss some practical points for praying with folks who are dealing with demonic oppression or possession. The following are principles I've gathered from my own experience of praying for folks and witnessing some breakthroughs. As with anything in life, both spiritual and mundane, it is wise to seek out more seasoned practitioners who can perhaps offer something like an apprenticeship in this area. Just be sure they are qualified by being well-grounded in God's Word.

1. **It is not usually wise to go it alone when praying for folks who seem to be dealing with influence from demons, especially when you first get started.** Get someone else to join you in prayer. There is power in numbers. Ecclesiastes 4:12 says, "Though one may be overpowered, two can defend themselves. A cord of three strands is not quickly broken." This is sage wisdom. Take someone with you.

2. **We don't have to yell at demons.** I know I told a story about praying loudly over a guy, but that was just me doing me. That wasn't a universal principle at work. Yelling doesn't create power or increase effectiveness. Authority is imparted by the Holy Spirit, not self-generated, and it is not activated by emotion. Of course, we may sometimes get angry at the evil we encounter, but our battling does not depend on how loud we are. Paul said our authority has more to do with our stand than our yell. "Therefore put on the full armor of God, so that when the day of evil comes, you may be able to stand your ground, and after you have done everything, to stand" (Eph. 6:13).

EXPOSING THE KINGDOM OF GOD

3. **Use the name of Jesus.** Paul said, "At the name of Jesus every knee should bow in heaven and on earth and under the earth" (Phil. 2:10). Every tongue will one day confess that Jesus is Lord. Even Jesus acknowledged that the demons knew him, though they didn't worship him. His name has power. As I write this, I have just prayed the name of Jesus over and over, while standing over someone who is dying. What better prayer could I have for someone leaving this life than the name of the One he will meet when he crosses from this life into Jesus' unhindered presence? His name is the most powerful word in the universe.

4. **Speak to Jesus.** Be very careful about this when engaged in spiritual warfare. I rarely address a demon directly. I reserve that for folks who have much more experience. Instead I let Jesus do the heavy lifting, asking him to release demons of all power. I ask that they be sent to him and for him to do with them as he will.

5. **Don't automatically assign every hurt, habit, or hang-up to the Enemy of your soul.** My inability to get any place on time is not the work of a demon. That's just me being too random as I think. The tickets I've gotten for speeding? Not the work of the Enemy. The wrecks I've had? Also not the Enemy. Too much dessert? You get the point. Not everything is the fault of Satan. Don't let that excuse rob someone of personal responsibility. Give the Enemy his due, but don't give him more power than he deserves.

LISTENING TO THE WORD

My recommendation, if you haven't had a lot of experience with casting out demons, is to simply ask Jesus to help you start where you are. Don't force it. Just ask Jesus to show you how to battle with darkness, and trust that he will do so in a way that works for you.

Group Gathering

OPEN WITH PRAYER

WATCH SESSION 6 VIDEO

DISCUSS THE FOLLOWING QUESTIONS BASED ON READINGS 26–30

26

Key Observation
Knowing the Enemy seems important if we are going to use the power and authority given us to defeat him.

Question for Discussion
How do you respond to this statement? How important do you believe it is that we understand the enemy of our souls?

27

Key Observation
I believe our sent-ness is to the same things that called the Israelites out of Egypt. It is a call to choose life and reject the powers of hell and death.

Question for Discussion
What has been your first-person experience of the demonic? And what do you most want to know?

28

Key Observation
The kingdom suffers the violence of a demonic world that has lost the war but continues to fight battles on its way to final, full defeat.

Question for Discussion
How do you respond to this statement? With belief? Curiosity? Doubt? Suspicion?

29

Key Observation
This is our trust. We have been entrusted with both the gospel and its expansion on earth. Spreading it means taking risks, crossing into enemy territory, being bold and courageous.

Question for Discussion
What does it look like in your context to be bold and courageous?

30

Key Observation
What is the mission of God's people? To connect with the heart of God, to share God's work of salvation and revelation, and to expose the kingdom of God and the cosmic reign of Jesus Christ over all things. In short, we exist to welcome and advance the kingdom of God.

Question for Discussion
How might a statement like this help in clarifying the work of the church? Of your church?

CLOSE WITH PRAYER

Jesus gave his followers power and authority to cast out demons. As you close this session in prayer, you're invited to name the demons that are pestering or possessing you or those you love. Spirits (or demons) of fear, anxiety, lust, anger, passivity, lying . . . all these spirits must submit to the name of Jesus. Where you see these spirits manifesting, speak the name of Jesus over them and ask him to remove anything that isn't fit for the kingdom of God.

SECTION

SEVEN

31

SHAKEN, NOT STIRRED

Key Observation
*What bothers lots of us is not **that** Jesus calls, but **how** he calls. We want to define terms before we take up calls, like Jesus is a waiter, not a Messiah.*

> **Read Luke 9:57–62.**
> - What do we know about the men described in this passage? Describe their relationship to Jesus. How does it compare with your relationship with Jesus?
> - List the three reasons these men gave for not being "all in" at the moment of their conversation with Jesus. Do you discern deeper motives? If so, name them.
> - What do you learn about Jesus from this scene? What do you learn about people? What do you learn about following Jesus?

These verses (Luke 9:57–62) challenge our willingness to go with God. It is interesting to note that not everyone who encountered Jesus was immediately compelled to follow him. Some, maybe most, didn't even realize when they were with him that they were standing in the presence of God incarnate. I think about the thousands upon thousands who walked right by Jesus every day—people who passed him in the marketplace, who met him in the temple, or who listened to him preach—who never knew they were with the Son of God.

How does that happen? How did they miss it?

Dr. Benjamin Pratt wrote an interesting book about James Bond, in which he considered the spiritual angle of James Bond stories. Ian Fleming, the

SUPERNATURAL

author of the James Bond novels, contended that the goal of the creation of the James Bond character was to write a series of parables about evil people. Pratt said Fleming used the seven deadly sins as a foundation for his characters. His favorite sin to write about? Accidie. The Oxford Dictionary of the Christian Church defines *accidie* as "a state of restlessness and inability either to work or to pray."[16] According to Fleming, it is the ultimate sin. In Pratt's book, he drew all kinds of meaning out of Fleming's use of that sin in the 007 novels.

Consider, for instance, James Bond's drink of choice. Do you happen to know what it was? It was a martini, "shaken not stirred."[17] Pratt believed Fleming chose that particular drink with the sin of accidie in mind. "In its fullest meaning accidie," he wrote, "refers to the loss of joy or faith in the goodness of life or the goodness of God."[18] In other words, it is to be shaken, but not stirred.

Now, I need to confess here: I don't know enough about James Bond or Ian Fleming to say whether or not the author was thinking that deeply when he made a "martini, shaken not stirred" Bond's drink of choice. But I am moved by this idea that there is a temptation, after we are shaken, *not to stir*. That sounds familiar. I suspect we've found a few guys here in Luke 9 who might have been interested in this good news if it had been more convenient. I suspect, too, that they have found a place in the Bible because they are us.

We are demonstrating this when we have that temptation to keep our Sunday disconnected from our Monday through Saturday, or to keep our small group disconnected from the rest of our lives. Or when we mindlessly read Scripture without letting it sink in and change us, or when we say a prayer but don't walk in faith as we stand up from it.

Shaken, not stirred.

> God does not want to make you comfortable. God wants to make you great.

It is all the people who would look for someone to blame rather than look for where God might be at work so they can join him. It is anyone who would rather have a theological debate than actually encounter the power of Jesus, the Christ. It is the one who wears the Christian T-shirt but never gets around to the deeper witness.

Shaken, not stirred.

It is any of us who would rather live in the land of "should do and ought to" than under the banner of the Great Commission.

Shaken, not stirred.

What bothers many of us is not *that* Jesus calls but *how* he calls. We wince at the timing of the call or the circumstances surrounding it, or we doubt the voice

SHAKEN, NOT STIRRED

we hear or the affirmation others give us when they assure us we have gifts for leadership. We fear change. Oh my, do we fear change!

We want to define terms before we take up this call, like Jesus is a waiter, not the Messiah. Why would normal people be put off by a display of kingdom power? Because it is inconvenient! Because it requires us to grow up and do grown-up things. Because it challenges our assumptions about God and because it makes us uncomfortable. In short, it requires us to change. But we learn a lesson from the three guys with excuses: Jesus is not asking us to follow him so we can be safe or do things that feel comfortable. Jesus is asking us to follow him so he can make us great. And by great, I mean faithful. Holy. Carrying power and authority.

Let me say that again: God does not want to make you comfortable. God wants to make you great. And not because you're capable of greatness, but because *he* is.

LISTENING TO THE WORD

Is there an invitation over your life right now? If so, how are you holding back from an enthusiastic yes? Is it in your giving? Your time to serve? Your obedience to follow through on a hard thing? Write out your best sense of what Jesus is inviting you into in this season of your life. Then beneath that statement, write this in red ink: "Follow me."

Now . . . respond.

32

BUT WHAT IF I DON'T WANT TO?

Key Observation
God has a plan for your life that probably involves a little plow-burning. It is likely less convenient than you're comfortable with and the task will probably take you to the edge of your competence and over it. This is especially true if you are feeling your way right now into a more vibrant supernatural expression of your faith in God.

Read Luke 9:62, then read 1 Kings 19:19–21.
- Compare these two passages.
- Using a Bible dictionary or commentary, do a little research on both Elijah and Elisha to find out more about their lives.
- Just so we're clear, who is doing the plowing? What does this teach us about Elisha?
- What do you think is the significance of the cloak that Elijah threw over Elisha's shoulders?

You can't beat 1 Kings 18 and 19 for intrigue and drama. It is an action-packed section that highlights the power of good over evil. King Ahab challenged Elijah to a duel of prophetic power, and Elijah won. Ahab and his wife Jezebel—poor losers—sent word that they were out to kill Elijah. Of course, the news is rough for Elijah; no one has their life threatened and comes out whistling. He wondered where God was. He felt alone and abandoned but on the other side of all his wrestling, he was more determined than ever to live for God.

BUT WHAT IF I DON'T WANT TO?

He began by going to find a young man named Elisha (the names can be confusing because they sound a lot alike, so pay attention). When Elijah found him, Elisha was plowing his field. In fact, he had twelve pairs of oxen plowing the field, so he must have been doing well for himself. Elisha was driving one pair of oxen himself when Elijah walked up, placed his cloak over his shoulders, and walked away.

This was quite a gesture. It would be like Andy Taylor taking off his sheriff's badge and pinning it to Barney Fife's uniform. Elijah was passing on his authority as a leader of God's people. He meant for Elisha to lay aside his old life and follow. Elisha ran to catch up with him, saying, "Let me kiss my father and mother goodbye" (1 Kings 19:20). Elijah was not amused. He responded, "What have I done to you?" (v. 20). In other words, "What have I done, that you won't receive this authority from me as a rare and treasured gift?"

Elisha got the hint, returned to his oxen, broke the plowing equipment into firewood, then slaughtered the oxen and barbecued it. Then Elisha "set out to follow Elijah and became his servant" (v. 21).

This is the story behind Jesus' words, "No one who puts a hand to the plow and looks back is fit for service in the kingdom of God" (Luke 9:62). The moral of Elisha's story and of the three examples in Luke 9 is that when God calls, we go. There can be no looking back.

> Can't we just keep going to church without stretching ourselves into new things? Well, yes, you can, but not if you want kingdom fruit from your efforts.

And I want to tell you right now that God has a plan for your life that probably involves a little plow-burning. It is likely less convenient than you're comfortable with, and the task will probably take you to the edge of your competence and over it. This is especially true if you are feeling your way right now into a more vibrant supernatural expression of your faith in God. That can feel unfamiliar and uncomfortable. *Can't we just keep going to church without stretching ourselves into new things?* Well, yes, you can, but not if you want kingdom fruit from your efforts.

The stories in Luke 9 of folks who wrestled with a call sound familiar, not just because we know them in our own lives but because similar stories chronicled in the Bible. Doesn't it help to know we're not any different than those great people who fostered the faith we now hold? These were people who were used mightily of God, and they also wrestled with his call to set their old life aside in order to follow him out to the radical edge of faith.

SUPERNATURAL

Real people who had a major impact on our faith also hesitated and doubted, worried and negotiated. They questioned whether it was God or indigestion from last night's food. Are you helped by that thought, like I am? I am glad to know on those days when I doubt God's call or try hard to ignore his voice that I am not alone in my struggle, that God is patient with people like me. That is a comfort.

One of the more powerful parts of this story in 1 Kings is the passing of the cloak—the mantle—from Elijah (think "senior prophet") to Elisha (think "junior prophet"). When Elijah truly came through his valley to the other side, his first response was to find a partner so he could pour into the next generation. He knew his work was not for him alone but for him to pass along. This is a good word for every one of us. We are all on one side or the other of that equation. We are either someone who needs to be poured into, or someone ready to pour into others. We may even be both!

Which are you? If you are ready to shift gears and follow Jesus into a new season, who are you inviting to lead you spiritually as you go? Who will inspire you to keep going deeper, and who will challenge you when you stall? If you have been on a journey for a while and have learned some things about how God works, who are you raising up to take up the next leg of the journey?

LISTENING TO THE WORD

> If you don't have a mentor, today is a good day for you to begin praying about who you could ask to be your mentor. Who out there inspires you to greater faith? Who is willing to go with you into the supernatural, where the kingdom of God is exposed? Ask God to give you a name, then get connected.

33

NO MORE UNHOLY HESITATION!

Key Observation
Whatever else we might guess, we can be sure of this: in the kingdom of God, there is no room for fear.

Read Genesis 19:1–26.
- This is a lengthy passage. Summarize it in your own words.
- From your reading of it, do you think Lot knew these were angels he had encountered at the gate? Why do you think they showed up to Lot? What was their purpose?
- Look at how verse 16 begins: "When he hesitated . . ." How does that phrase connect with themes we found in 1 Kings 19 or Luke 9?
- Think about hesitation for a moment (pun intended). When is it a sign of integrity and wisdom? When is it a sign of a lack of faith?
- What was the angels' advice to the family as they fled (see v. 17)? Why do you suppose not looking back was important?
- How does that advice—"don't look back"—connect with what you've read in Luke 9 or 1 Kings 19?

I'm confident there are times when our hesitations are holy. Sometimes it is the wiser course to stop and count the cost, rather than reacting too quickly out of emotion. The Bible repeatedly advises us to "wait on the Lord" (Ps. 7:14 NKJV; Ps. 37:9 NKJV; Ps. 37:34 NKJV; Isa. 40:31 NKJV). That's pure wisdom. Sometimes the waiting sanctifies us.

SUPERNATURAL

But sometimes hesitation is a sign of unholy fear. Sometimes it is us hesitating at God's call because we struggle to embrace change. And sometimes we shrink back from the nudge to pray deliverance or healing over someone. But remember a verse in Hebrews: "We do not belong to those who shrink back and are destroyed, but to those who have faith and are saved" (10:39). People who follow Jesus do not live in the camp of those who shrink back!

> A focus on ourselves, on the preservation of our own comforts and securities, on what is familiar and comfortable will kill the human spirit and stifle the Holy Spirit.

When I was a little girl, I had really bad nightmares. I would wake up petrified and run for my parents' room. I wanted my mother's comfort. But it was dark, and things in the dark look ominous. If there was anything on the floor of their bedroom—clothes, bedroom shoes, anything that could be misinterpreted in the dark—I would end up standing paralyzed in the doorway, just feet from their bed, unable to reach my mom for fear of what that thing on the floor might be. I always assumed the worst.

Whatever happened in my childhood carried over into my grown-up life and created a fear-based response to a lot of things in my adulthood. I didn't admit fear, but I would respond to opportunities with an overdeveloped need for control. Maybe you can relate. If you've had wounds in your childhood, that carries over and translates into fear-based responses in adulthood. We can become afraid of getting too close to people, afraid of losing control, afraid of going too far with God, and maybe even afraid of succeeding (too much pressure!).

So we start to bargain. We say to ourselves or to God, "I'll get serious about my faith when I get a family or when I finish college or after I get the right job with the right days off so I can really pour myself into my faith." The Enemy of our souls just loves that fear-based hesitation. Paralyzing fear takes away our power to fight the Enemy.

In Romans 7:15, Paul wrote, "I do not understand what I do. For what I want to do I do not do, but what I hate I do." I love finding lines like this one in the Bible because they remind me that God understands us. He gets human nature. He gets that we do things we wish we didn't do. He gets that sometimes we are going to hesitate when we ought to move forward. That sometimes we are going to relapse when we ought to stay sober. That sometimes we are going to promise ourselves we will never do (fill in the blank) again, and then we go and do that very thing.

NO MORE UNHOLY HESITATION!

Many of the things we do that we hate have their roots in the spirit of fear. We fear death, we fear pain, we fear failure, we fear being seen as a failure, and we fear being uncomfortable. And, oh my goodness, do we hate change!

Perhaps this is why the angels warned Lot's family as they did. The end of this story is full of tragedy. Two cities are destroyed because of the evil within, and a woman is killed for looking back as she ran. This is a bizarre end to a bizarre story. Surely there was more to the action of Lot's wife than simply looking backward as she ran. What was it in her spirit or attitude that caught the attention of God? Why did that disobedience require her life?

Whatever else we might guess, we can be sure of this: in the kingdom of God, there is no room for fear. John said, in fact, that "perfect love drives out fear" (1 John 4:18). To the extent that we operate from fear, we will miss the very love, power, and call of God to expose his kingdom through our lives. And we will miss it while we're trying to protect ourselves, proving Jesus' point in Luke 9:24: "Whoever wants to save their life will lose it."

In short, focusing on self will destroy us. A focus on ourselves, on the preservation of our own comforts and securities, on what is familiar and comfortable will kill the human spirit and stifle the Holy Spirit.

Do you want to go with God? Die to self. Cast out the spirit of fear. Let there be no more unholy hesitation!

LISTENING TO THE WORD

In your life, where are the unholy hesitations, whether hesitating in the presence of a call or hesitating to break a habit? Where do you need to be moving forward, not looking backward? Make a list of everything you hear, then pray through it for healing and deliverance.

34

JESUS PLANS TO WRECK YOUR LIFE

Key Observation
Jesus plans to wreck your life.

Read Luke 14:15–24, then read Luke 9:57–62 again.

- Compare the excuses found in Luke 14 with those found in Luke 9. How are they similar? How are they different?
- Compare the reaction of the master in Luke 14 to the reaction of Jesus in Luke 9.
- Jesus invites people in Luke 9 to follow; how would Luke 14 define that "following"? In other words, what is the servant charged with doing in Luke 14? How does that inform your understanding of what it means to follow Jesus?

I don't know about you, but I keep getting stuck on one point as we journey through this study. I keep returning to the sad fact that so many missed Jesus when he showed up. We wondered in the story of the feeding of the five thousand if there were people in that crowd who completely missed the miracle. We were warned by Jesus himself that some would not accept the disciples when they went out to the towns and villages. And here in this week's passage, we see people hedging on their decision to follow him.

What must it be like to have Jesus himself standing before me, only to miss the glory of him, the truth of him, the invitation? What must it be like to have

JESUS PLANS TO WRECK YOUR LIFE

Jesus' call to follow and then to look back rather than forge ahead? I need to tell you that obedience will put you in some uncomfortable places. It will take you beyond logic and will ask you to keep stepping out, step-by-step, while the ground rises to meet you one step at a time. But listen, *it is step-by-step*, which is not complicated. Fear is what makes it feel complicated, but obedience is not actually that complicated.

> Obedience will put you in some uncomfortable places. It will take you beyond logic and will ask you to keep stepping out, step-by-step, while the ground rises to meet you one step at a time.

Did you know the very first bungee jumper didn't actually mean to? As the story goes, it was a woman living on Pentecost Island (That's an irony, isn't it?). She was trying to escape her husband, who was beating her, so she climbed a tree. He yelled at her to come down and told her that if she came down he would only beat her a little, but if he had to climb up there after her, she would be sorry.

She didn't come down.

So he climbed up but just as he got to her, she jumped. In the confusion of that moment, he jumped, too, not realizing that while he had been climbing the tree she had been tying vines to her ankles. Consequently, she survived that jump but he didn't. Ever since, for generations now, the men of Pentecost Island have made an annual practice of jumping out of trees. Only they jump like the girl, with vines tied to their ankles.[19]

Bungee jumping is scary, but it is not complicated. Bungee jumping consists, basically, of three things. Tie one end of an elastic rope to your ankle. Fix the other end of the rope to a high structure. Jump.

That's it, and it's not complicated. And isn't this the same basic pattern for faith? Attach one end of a belief system to yourself. Attach the other end to a very high structure (say, God). Then, jump.

That, simply put, is faith. In other words, it is believing that if we jump, we won't hit the pavement. The writer of Hebrews taught that faith is praying that which is not as if it is, and that faith is not the product of striving because faith is not that complicated. Fear is what makes it feel complicated, but obedience—the action word for faith—is actually not that complicated. Just make sure you are attached at both ends before you jump.

Remember? We do not belong to the camp of those who shrink back. We belong to those who have faith and are saved. Jesus said that in the last days, the people who are busy protecting their own lives and lifestyles will end up without a place

> SUPERNATURAL

at the table while those who live in the margins will have a place of honor at the banquet. The point is that Jesus will keep drawing folks in and will always look for those who give a holy yes to the call to go out and find the next ones.

And this is where Luke 9 ultimately leads us. It leads us right into Luke 10, where we discover that where we started in Luke 9 (people being sent out to cast out demons, cure diseases, proclaim the kingdom, and heal the sick) starts over again in Luke 10 as seventy-two others are sent out. This is the pattern of kingdom ministry. We go out into the fields, find those who are open to the gospel, disciple them as followers of Jesus, then send them out to find others just like them. This is what it means to follow Jesus.

Do you get it yet, that Jesus doesn't intend to invite you into the kingdom without changing your life? That was never part of the deal. It doesn't matter which side of the equation you're on. Whether you are part of the family being called out into the world, or you're some broken, messed-up person ripe for healing or deliverance. Either way, Jesus plans to wreck your life.

Let me just say that again: Jesus plans to wreck your life.

LISTENING TO THE WORD

Pray for those in your life who are suffering from their own unholy hesitations when it comes to living a surrendered life. And pray the boldest of prayers, that Jesus would wreck your life and do something completely new with you.

35

BUT FIRST . . .

Key Observation
A "but first" mentality that is always putting off the deeper things of God until we have control over everything else is the mentality of death.

> ### Read Luke 9:57–62 one more time, then read Matthew 6:33–34.
> - When you read the passage in Luke 9, this time notice the conditions placed on the disciples' following. What do you notice about how those conditions are worded?
> - What is the connection between this passage in Luke and the passage in Matthew?
> - Try this exercise: Read each excuse offered in Luke, one at a time, and each time follow it by the two verses in Matthew. Does that help you to hear more clearly Jesus' point in Luke 9?

Maybe I'm projecting and you're all about supernatural ministry and don't have the first hesitation about jumping in with both feet. But on the off chance that you're still finding all kinds of reasons to do Bible study *about* supernatural things as a way of avoiding actually getting out there and *doing* supernatural things, I figure studying this passage is worth one more chapter. I'm hoping this will sink in—that all those excuses we have all made over and over in order to maintain the status quo, they won't work with Jesus.

Let's just review the stories of these three guys one more time. The first guy seemed more ready to go than Jesus was to take him. The interesting thing about this guy is that on the surface he seemed ready to go with Jesus. This guy tells us something about ourselves that is hard to hear: even when we don't admit it to ourselves and Jesus, there are parts of us that are deathly afraid of not having every need covered before we step out. And that kind of hedging is no use to the kingdom because paralyzing fear takes away our power to fight the Enemy.

The second guy in this passage just asked to take care of his dying father first. Seems reasonable, right? It seems a little callous of Jesus to ask a guy to walk away from a dying man. Scholars debate what was really going on here, whether this is about a guy's inheritance or just the need to be the one calling the shots at his father's death; either way, the real point is that our control issues show up in the relationships we emphasize. Whether that relationship is money or family issues, it can be sneaky because it doesn't seem like control but seems like common sense or being responsible.

> Your best and highest thought for your own life doesn't come close to Jesus' best and highest thought for your life.

But this—exactly here, where we must wrestle with what we emphasize—Jesus said, is where we have to decide what has our hearts. You can't serve both God and *anything*. Look at verse 60 again, where Jesus said, "Let the dead bury their own dead, *but you go and proclaim the kingdom of God*" (emphasis added). In other words, compared to the kingdom of God, everything else is dust and ashes. Whether it is your father or your inheritance or your retirement fund or your closest and most important relationships, here is the truth: if you want peace, all the rest of it has to find its place inside the kingdom of God.

And then there is the guy who just needs a minute to say goodbye to his family. The key words in this one are "but first" (v. 61). Because this is where most of us live. We want to surrender all of it . . . *but first*. *But first*, let me raise my kids. *But first*, let me get a better income. *But first*, let me get a better work schedule. *But first*, let me get a little more comfortable with praying out loud, laying hands on people, and talking about supernatural things. *But first* . . . and before we can finish, Jesus points us right back to the kingdom of God.

Because here's the thing. The stuff you do to control the people and circumstances in your life will not work with Jesus. You cannot be passive aggressive with Jesus and tell him you want to follow him while inside you hold on to all your stuff. You can even argue with him and bargain with him, but there will be no controlling him. Jesus will not have it. Why? Because Jesus knows you better than you know yourself. Your best and highest thought for your own life doesn't come close to Jesus' best and highest thought for your life. And after you've surrendered your worries and anxieties and your need to control everything, after all those things are gone, God will remain.

BUT FIRST...

And God will not be controlled.

Matthew 6:33–34 is the punch line for all Jesus said in Luke. Never mind the details; pursue the kingdom and let God handle the rest. Why? Because when we start by controlling the circumstances, we end up being controlled by them, but when we start with the kingdom of God, everything else falls in line behind it. This is what happens when we choose surrender over control. We discover what is most important. We will deal with our trust issues. We will be messier and be okay with it. We will experience spiritual freedom because the real freedom is in surrender.

The "but first..." mentality—that is always putting off the deeper things of God until we have control over everything else—is the mentality of death. I want to say that with more subtlety, but there is no kinder, gentler way to get at this truth. Believe me when I tell you, as one beggar telling another beggar where to find bread, there is no "but first..." in the kingdom. Just *go!*

LISTENING TO THE WORD

Think of something you're living with right now that is a cause for anxiety. Where in your life do you say, *I'll do this thing for Jesus, but first*... Admit that, and begin asking God to help you repent of it. If you can't repent, then pray, "Repent me." That is a prayer that admits you can't change yourself and acknowledges that Jesus must do the changing in you.

Group Gathering

OPEN WITH PRAYER

WATCH SESSION 7 VIDEO

DISCUSS THE FOLLOWING QUESTIONS BASED ON READINGS 31–35

31

Key Observation
*What bothers lots of us is not **that** Jesus calls, but **how** he calls. We want to define terms before we take up calls, like Jesus is a waiter, not a Messiah.*

Question for Discussion
How have you experienced the call of God? How would you characterize that experience—as jarring, unexpected, hard, challenging, gentle, joyful, a relief, or something else?

32

Key Observation
God has a plan for your life that probably involves a little plow-burning. It is likely less convenient than you're comfortable with and the task will probably take you to the edge of your competence and over it. This is especially true if you are feeling your way right now into a more vibrant supernatural expression of your faith in God.

Question for Discussion
What plows in your field probably need to be burned in order for you to go with God? Be as specific as you can.

33

Key Observation
Whatever else we might guess, we can be sure of this: in the kingdom of God, there is no room for fear.

Question for Discussion
Where are you making room for fear in your life? And how do you need to repent of that?

34

Key Observation
Jesus plans to wreck your life.

Question for Discussion
Are you okay with that? If not, why not? And if so, what does that likely mean for you?

35

Key Observation
A "but first" mentality that is always putting off the deeper things of God until we have control over everything else is the mentality of death.

Question for Discussion
In your own life, how might putting off the deeper things of God actually breed death into your existence? Think creatively about this idea.

CLOSE WITH PRAYER

Pray especially against the spirit of passivity where it exists in your life, in the life of your church, and in the life of the church as a whole. Pray against any spirit that would seek to leave us comfortably numb. Ask for the Lord to give you a hunger for the supernatural and a thirst for real life. If anyone in your group needs to confess this spirit of passivity, come around this one and pray for a spiritual hunger to invade.

SECTION EIGHT

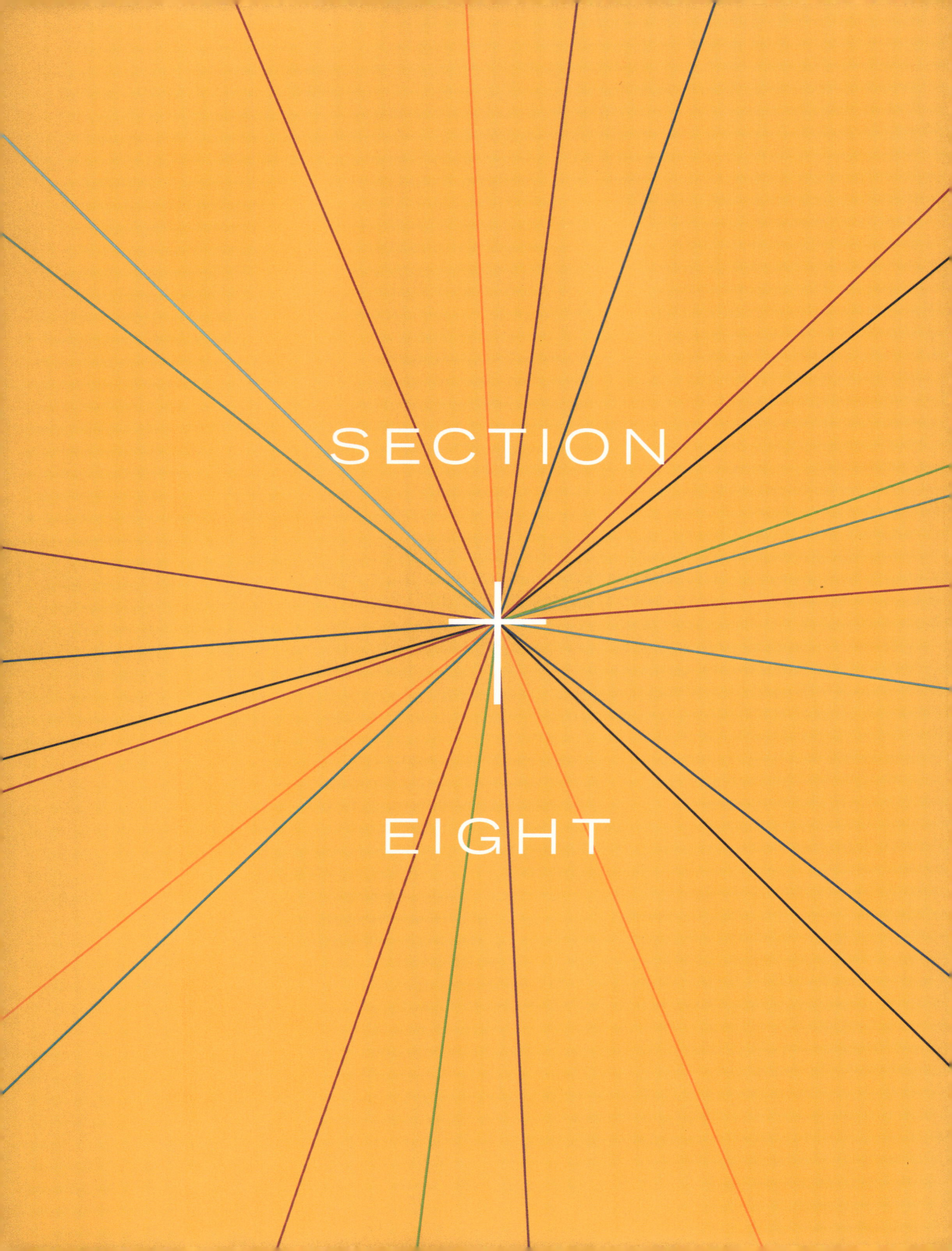

36

LIVE THIS

Key Observation
This is what it means to be sent. It means bearing fruit. It means recognizing that the kingdom keeps moving and that we are called to move with it, in the footsteps of Jesus, our Apostle and High Priest.

> **Read through the whole chapter of Luke 9 in one sitting. It is even better if you can read it out loud.**
> - Remember what you've studied so far. What stands out for you this time around?
> - What do you notice about the disciples? What do you notice about Jesus? What pressures do you sense they faced? What fears, worries, freedoms, and/or strengths did they show?

After a panoramic look across the ministry of Jesus, we land in the first verses of Luke 10, where Jesus was again sending people out to harvest souls. Harvesting souls is the power of the gospel and the heart of it. Luke 9—an action-packed, day-in-the-life snapshot of a disciple's life in the company of God's only begotten Son—is a great chapter to study because it spreads before us such a variety of ways Jesus and his followers live it out.

One night, years ago, when I first sat down with my Bible and a notebook to begin this study of Luke 9, I was of course riveted by Jesus in this one chapter: he was sending out disciples, feeding five thousand people, foretelling his death two times, seeing Moses and Elijah, healing people, and explaining the high cost of discipleship. But the disciples' lives were also stunning: how far out on the edge they lived and how unsafe their lives were as followers of Jesus. There were no perfectionists among those followers but also no wimps. So much of what they did was accomplished in the crucible of doubt, fear, and uncertainty—a kind of hopeful, messy, edgy adventurism.

SUPERNATURAL

Reading Luke 9 that first time through, I started a list and ended up with forty things followers do, or at least forty things those hopeful, messy, edgy followers did in a season when they were remarkably fruitful. This list of habits from imperfect but faithful followers will both encourage and inspire you if you are struggling to answer the question, When I follow Jesus, what do I *do*? This list includes some things that all Jesus' followers did in Luke 9, as well as some things that only the three followers did, who followed him onto the mountain.

1. They come when Jesus calls.
2. They accept power and authority given by Jesus.
3. They go where he sends.
4. They talk about the kingdom of God.
5. They heal people.
6. They depend exclusively on his resources (and don't get sidetracked by their own needs).
7. They follow Jesus' instructions.
8. They talk to Jesus about what it's like to follow his lead.
9. They go off with him to rest after serving.
10. They come to him with ideas and questions.
11. They have conversations with him.
12. They tell him what they have and don't have.
13. They do what he says, even when they don't understand.
14. They pray with him in private.
15. They talk to him about how they see the world.
16. They talk to him about how they see him.
17. They express their belief in him.
18. They keep quiet about things he shares with them when he asks them to.
19. They listen when he talks about the future.
20. Some of them will go away with him to pray.
21. Some of them will see him in his glorified body.
22. Some of them are enveloped by God's glory.
23. Some of them are afraid of what they experience when they are with him.
24. Some of them hear the voice of God.
25. Some of them will have dramatic spiritual experiences they won't talk about.
26. Some of them will experience dramatic spiritual things but will be asked to move on from it.
27. Some of them will attempt to drive out demons and fail.
28. They see Jesus get frustrated by perversion and unbelief.
29. They step aside and watch Jesus heal people.
30. They hear Jesus but don't understand.
31. They are afraid to ask Jesus questions.
32. They argue among themselves.
33. They compete with one another for greatness.
34. They try to stop people outside their group from doing things in the name of Jesus.

LIVE THIS

35. They are admonished by Jesus when they try to stop people from doing things in his name.
36. Some are sent ahead of Jesus to prepare the way for him.
37. They ask Jesus for permission to be vengeful. (Note: permission for this was denied.)
38. They walk with him.
39. They promise to follow Jesus wherever he goes, without fully understanding the cost of that commitment.
40. They hear his call to follow but tend to put conditions on obedience.

> Never once did Jesus command people to go find a big room where they sit passively to receive. But every day, he called people to *be* the church—to serve him together as a community of healed, saved, and delivered people who are hungry to see others healed, saved, and delivered.

This is what it means to follow Jesus, and from the first invitation Jesus gave to the first disciple (see Luke 5:1–11), Jesus has been inviting folks out into this world. Or more accurately, *sending* them. Followers of Jesus are sent people. Jesus is essentially saying, "You are called to this . . . now *go*! Preach the gospel, cure diseases, heal the sick, and deliver people from their demons. Contend for the gospel and raise up others to do the same." This is what it means to be sent. It means bearing fruit. It means recognizing that the kingdom keeps moving and that we are called to move with it, in the footsteps of Jesus, our Apostle and High Priest.

Never once did Jesus command people to go find a big room where they sit passively to receive. But every day, he called people to *be* the church—to serve him together as a community of healed, saved, and delivered people who are hungry to see others healed, saved, and delivered. And every day, Jesus lived a supernatural lifestyle.

How does that compare with your experience of the Christian life?

LISTENING TO THE WORD

Is the list missing anything you want to add? Highlight items in the list that are especially meaningful to you. In prayer, take time to talk with God about the items you've highlighted. Ask him for greater understanding and revelation around these characteristics of a follower. Ask him to equip you to become all he'd have you become.

37

BEING SENT WITH LIVING WATER

Key Observation
To be an apostolic church is to believe that what we hold has been given to us to carry forward. We have both a call and a commission. We are sent people.

Read Luke 9:1–2 and Luke 10:1–3.
- Compare these two passages. How are they similar? How are they different?
- From these two passages, what do you learn about Jesus, about being sent out by Jesus, about people, and about the kingdom of God?

Somewhere online I found this little gem. The Greek word for *apostle* and the Latin word for *missionary* mean exactly the same thing: "sent one." To be an apostle is to be a missionary. Not all missionaries are apostles, of course, but I suspect that all who have the apostolic gifting are designed to be missional. To be an apostolic church is to believe that what we hold has been given to us to carry forward. We have both a call *and* a commission. We are sent people.

To be an apostolic church assumes fruitfulness, faithfulness, and a forward-thinking posture. It assumes confidence in the face of a questionable future. It assumes that our sent-ness is never revoked and certainly not just because it feels uncomfortable.

BEING SENT WITH LIVING WATER

Sent-ness is a funny thing. Being sent out doesn't usually create immediate gratification, nor does it come with enough credentials to make us confident in the going. More often, we're sent out feeling pretty incompetent to do something we may or may not see fruit from for days or weeks or months or often . . . *years*. And even then, we may find out that what we thought would be the fruit of a spiritual project doesn't end up being the real story at all!

Take King Hezekiah, for instance. Hezekiah was an Old Testament king who honored the Lord and had a pretty remarkable impact on a nation. In one generation he managed to turn a nation from godless and chaotic to faithful and prospering—*in one generation* (Don't we long for that kind of leader today?).

For all he did for the nation of Israel, it is interesting to note that during several mentions of Hezekiah, his construction of an aqueduct (a tunnel for carrying water) and a pool is emphasized. We might wonder why, when his obvious accomplishment was returning Israel to God in one generation, the Bible most often credits him as the guy who built a water system and a pool. Why does that matter?

My mentor helped me understand it. He said having water inside the walls of a desert city meant that when the city was under attack, the people could survive for a long time on the water inside the walls. Hezekiah's genius move was not building a bigger army or a better governmental system. It was making sure the people inside the walls could withstand any attack over a long period of time. By building an aqueduct, Hezekiah ensured that the people of God could persevere within the walls for the long haul. What a powerful gift to give a community!

> That work of digging the spiritual aqueduct and establishing the full pool of resources must happen day in and day out in the hidden place of prayer and Scripture study. This is where God digs deep wells within and where the Holy Spirit fills.

Folks, it is not good Bible-study method to allegorize historical events (in other words, to turn them into fables with good moral lessons), but sometimes there is an eternal principle at work in a historic event that ties the story of God together from cover to cover. The principle of Hezekiah's accomplishment is this: the water inside the walls is what gives us the internal resources to persevere. The water inside the walls sustains us.

In other words, give what God gives you.

No wonder Jesus sent out his first missionary evangelists with the instruction to take nothing with them—no staff, no bag, no bread, no money, no extra shirt. If you read on in Luke 10, you'll find he gave the same instruction to the next wave of "sent ones": *take nothing with you*. Why? Because he didn't want them to be tempted to give what I want to call "water outside the wall." What Jesus wanted them to depend on was the Holy Spirit within them, the living water of the gospel. That is the water that sustains people under siege and the water that quenches thirst and the water that heals. Because we've been told not to rely on ourselves or anything outside ourselves, it leaves us with nothing but what has quenched our own thirst and healed our own wounds. In the name of Jesus, we are sent out to share *that* living water. Nothing else.

Think a bit more deeply about water *within* the walls and water *outside* the walls. Water outside the walls might be our talents or the gifts and talents of others on whom we rely. It might be our external resources (money, for instance), or the simple fact that life is going well for us. Those externals can create a sense of strength. There is nothing wrong with that, unless of course it replaces our need for God. If we think we've got it all together—"I'll take it from here, Jesus"—we put ourselves in a spiritually vulnerable place, and not in a good way.

Water within the walls is a metaphor for the growing spiritual life. When we have living water with us—the Holy Spirit—we can be sustained even through long dry spells or difficult crises. When the Enemy comes at us, we've got resources within to fight the battles. We aren't defenseless.

Of course, the time for developing water within the walls is not the day the Enemy shows up. That work of digging the spiritual aqueduct and establishing the full pool of resources must happen day in and day out in the hidden place of prayer and Scripture study. This is where God digs deep wells within and where the Holy Spirit fills.

LISTENING TO THE WORD

How are you digging your own spiritual waterlines so you always have "water within the walls" when you need it? What spiritual disciplines sustain you? What disciplines do you need to commit (or recommit) to?

38

DO IT AGAIN

Key Observation
A testimony defeats the Enemy by changing the spiritual climate. It unleashes possibilities. It unleashes the "do it again" power of the miracle you're witnessing to.

> **Read Luke 10:1–3 again, then read Revelation 12:10–11.**
> - Who are the seventy-two? Why do you think he sent them out in pairs? Why do you think he sent them to places he also planned to visit?
> - Just so we are clear on it, define "harvest" as it is used here.
> - Think down the road and give your best guess for these questions: What happens when there are finally enough workers for all the fields? What happens when the harvest is completed?
> - According to Revelation 12, how was the Enemy defeated?

We have forgotten—too many of us—that this good news is not ours. This good news is ours to share. If you have received that glorious release from shame and guilt, then it becomes yours to give to the next person. If you've been healed, then you are healed to become a healer. If you've been set free by knowing the truth, then that becomes your story to share. If that place inside of you that's been dead for years is being brought to life again, or if that relationship that you thought was dead is being restored, then you have received this as a gift. And the Word says, what we have freely received, we are to freely give (see Matthew 10:8).

Did you know that the word *testimony* in the Bible actually means "witness," "return," and "do again"? It can also mean something like "a warning." Combine those meanings and you get something profound. When we share our stories of salvation, of healing, or of God's miraculous or redemptive work in our lives, it

SUPERNATURAL

is as if we are returning to that moment and bringing that power forward into the present. *We are giving God an opportunity to show up again.*

Years ago, when I was first learning the art of healing prayer, I would practice it together with a friend who was also just learning. We would get together and practice praying over each other. It was in those sessions with my friend that I received my first immediate, miraculous healing through prayer. God revealed to me the source of some significant unresolved anger and rebellion, and in a moment I was set free. It was amazing, and it changed my life.

On the same day as that healing, I had a lunch appointment with someone. I'd just had this huge healing moment, so I was sort of floating by the time I hit that restaurant. My whole story of healing bubbled over onto the person I was having lunch with. I told her how I'd been healed of this bitter spirit and while I was telling my story, something was unleashed in her. Emphatically, she said, "I want that." I said, "Well, okay . . . when I learn how I'll let you know."

But she was adamant, saying, "No! I want that now!" Right then, we went back to the church and I prayed over her. I had no idea what I was doing, but I didn't have the guts to tell her so. I prayed, asking God to take her back to the moment when the Enemy first spoke a lie into her life. Then we waited for the Spirit to move. It seemed to me like nothing was happening. Just about the time I was beginning to wonder just who I thought I was, trying something like this, she looked up at me from her place of prayer and said, "Now I know the power that raised Lazarus from the dead."

> **If you've been healed, then you are healed to become a healer.**

I was stunned! Evidently right then, right there, she'd been touched by the power of God. The healing was immediate and real, and it was proven by how she responded in the days that followed. Relationships that had been broken for decades were completely restored. For years afterward, she could testify over and over that she was actually, fully, really healed.

And it started with my story.

Stories are powerful tools in the hands of God. They reveal the heart of God for us—his redemptive, promise-keeping heart. If we are saved by Jesus, we have touched the heart of the Father. When we talk about the saving work of Jesus in our own lives, we are exposing the heart of the Father for people.

Folks, your story has power because the God who wrote your story has power. Revelation 12:10–11 teaches us that the Enemy is defeated by two things: the blood of the Lamb and the power of the testimony. The Enemy is defeated first by when we claim the power of the blood of Jesus over our lives, and then again when we tell our story. A testimony defeats the Enemy by changing the spiritual climate. It unleashes possibilities. It unleashes the "do it again" power of the miracle we're witnessing to.

There is nothing better than being with a little kid who loves being with you—being on a playground with them, pushing them high on the swing set, listening to them laugh. Then when you stop and they still want to keep going, they scream with delight, "Do it again!" Every time we share our story, it is us saying to God, "Do it again!"

Yes, Lord, yes! Do it again!

LISTENING TO THE WORD

A testimony is simply who you were, what happened to change you, and who you are now. It can be a salvation story, or it can be like the story I told my friend during lunch that day. It can be a story of healing or deliverance or provision or even the story of how God held on when you felt like running. Take a few minutes now to write your story.

39

GO!

Key Observation
Never forget who you are. You are a follower of Jesus who has been given power and authority to cast out all demons, to cure diseases, to proclaim the kingdom of God, and to heal the things that destroy people's lives.

Read Luke 9:51–56.
- Why does the author connect the impending time of Jesus' death with this trip to Jerusalem? What does that imply that Jesus knew?
- Take note of the disciples who asked the question about fire. These were two of Jesus' first followers. What does that teach you?
- Do you think James and John had experience with raining down fire from heaven? Or were they expecting Jesus to do as they suggested?
- When Jesus rebuked someone, how do you think it sounded? Angry? Gentle? Firm?

Before we close, we need to explore one last tidbit in Luke 9 that we haven't yet addressed. It is a line that isn't actually there, at least not in the earliest manuscripts. A guy they didn't know was casting out demons, and Jesus' followers asked Jesus to put a stop to it. They actually had the nerve to ask Jesus if they could rain fire down on a few heads. Jesus was not a fan of that idea.

Look at Luke 9:55–56 again: "Jesus turned and rebuked them. Then he and his disciples went to another village." That is the New International Version of this passage, and the one you find in most Bibles today. But somewhere along the way some scribe felt the need to add a line between verses 55 and 56 of Luke 9. Scholars give it about an average chance of being an actual word from Jesus, and since it doesn't show up in the earliest manuscripts, you won't find it in most Bibles. When you add in the extra (or missing) sentence, the passage reads,

But He turned and rebuked them, [and said, "You do not know what kind of spirit you are of; for the Son of Man did not come to destroy men's lives, but to save them."] And they went on to another village. (NASB)

What a powerful commentary! Even if Jesus didn't say it here, he said it often. We follow Jesus, not because we do not know who Jesus is but because *we do not know who we are*. We do not even know what we are made of. We don't even have a clue how divided our lives are now or what kind of spirit we have access to. We are not aware most of the time what kind of power we have to go out and change the world.

We have bought some lie that the spirit of Jesus is a spirit of rules and condemnation and guilt, but it turns out that the spirit of Jesus is a spirit of redemption and deliverance. And we have been invited to give what we have been given so that by the authority of Christ and under the power of the Holy Spirit the kingdom of God will multiply to overflowing.

The Son of Man didn't come to destroy lives but to save them. Isn't that glorious news?

Mark Buchanan talked about visiting the famous Tuesday night prayer meeting at Brooklyn Tabernacle in New York. Thousands of people had been gathering there every Tuesday night for years. Buchanan called it "3,500 God-hungry people storming heaven for two hours."[20] On the Tuesday he went, he had dinner with Jim Cymbala, the pastor. Mark told a story of that dinner conversation, saying,

> *In the course of the meal, Jim turned to me and said, "Mark, do you know what the number one sin of the church in America is? . . . It's not the plague of internet pornography that is consuming our men. It's not that the divorce rate in the church is roughly the same as society at large. . . . The number one sin of the church in America," he said, "is that its pastors and leaders are not on their knees crying out to God, 'Bring us the drug-addicted, bring us the prostitutes, bring us the destitute, bring us the gang leaders, bring us those with AIDS, bring us the people nobody else wants, whom only you can heal, and let us love them in your name until they are whole.'"*[21]

In the face of such a statement, Mark Buchanan said he had no response because he had never prayed like that. So that night, he went home, repented, and began to cry out for those whom nobody wants.

> **There are fields full of people who desperately need someone who will claim the power of Christ over their broken lives, fields full of people whose salvation story has not yet been told.**

SUPERNATURAL

There is no shortage of those people; the fields are full of them, Jesus said. There are fields full of people who desperately need someone who will claim the power of Christ over their broken lives, fields full of people whose salvation story has not yet been told. There are billions of people still out there who haven't been reached, who more than anything need a fair account of the gospel and a generous dose of grace. There are untold numbers of people who are quietly suffering from childhood wounds and pestering demons, who don't even know what they are missing, for they simply endure the pain. And, friends, we have been given power and authority to go out and make a profound, even eternal, difference in those lives.

It is a high calling to be one who improves someone else's worth simply by a willingness to be present to them. Surely this is the work of real followers of Jesus: to redefine those we meet and help them understand their worth in light of their relationship with Christ.

To help someone see who they really are? That changes everything.

Never forget who you are. You are a child of the Most High God. You are a follower of Jesus who has been given power and authority to cast out all demons, to cure diseases, to proclaim the kingdom of God, and to heal the things that destroy people's lives.

LISTENING TO THE WORD

Who is God asking you to cry out for? The poor? The brokenhearted? The prisoners? Whose salvation story has not yet been told? Make your list, start praying, take authority, take the gospel, and go!

40

RECEIVE THE HOLY SPIRIT

Key Observation
Jesus will not stop sending people like us until the kingdom comes and God's will is done on earth as it is in heaven.

> **Read Luke 9:21–22.**
> - Again, we find Jesus warning folks not to tell anyone who he is. Why?
> - How did Jesus know he must suffer? How did he describe suffering in this passage?
> - What is the end result of so much suffering for Jesus? What is the end result of suffering for us, if it is done for the cause of Christ . . . or even when it is self-imposed pain redeemed by Christ?

When Jesus ascended into heaven after his resurrection, he sent the Holy Spirit, and the Holy Spirit's work is to build the church on earth. By revealing Jesus Christ as the Messiah of the world, the Holy Spirit builds churches. Why? Because God has chosen the church as his primary vehicle for saturating the world with the gospel. That's why, in much of the world, the church is a very dangerous idea.

In so many other places in the world, church folks are not arguing over why the youth group used the Crock-Pot to make cheese dip (yes, this happened in my church). In most places in the world, church folks are, every day, waking up prepared to die. Yet no other religion is growing at the rate of Christianity. Compare that with atheism, the only belief system that has declined.[22] In fact, the most persecuted countries are seeing the greatest rate of growth in Christianity. The church pours hope into the world because the church preaches Jesus, who is the hope of the world.

SUPERNATURAL

Despite what it must feel like in our own culture some days, the church is holding her own.

Timothy Tennent has served every summer for several decades in north India as a teacher and as part of a team that plants churches. This team has seen hundreds of churches planted in tribal areas, and often what they use to introduce the gospel is a film called *The Jesus Film*. If you've ever seen an Indian film, you know that it always has dancing, a lot of dancing. *The Jesus Film* has no dancing (go figure), so it struggled to hold people's attention in India. To make it work there, they had to throw in some dancing.

Yes, this movie about Jesus now has a "dance" version. When they showed this film in Bhopal, an audience with no knowledge of Jesus watched the whole story unfold—the miracles, the teachings, the demons being cast out, and of course, the dancing.

Then came the moment when Jesus was crucified and hung up on a cross. When he declared, "It is finished," the organizers of this gathering were taken by surprise. The people began to get up to go home. They'd heard the word "finished," and seen the main character die. What could be left?

But the story wasn't over! The organizers had to corral the audience back to their seats for the rest of the film. The people continued to watch. They saw the grief of the disciples, the women coming to the garden on the first day of the week to dress the body, the empty tomb, and the angels saying, "He is not here. He is risen." Then the resurrected Jesus appeared, and Dr. Tennent said he'd never seen anything like it. The whole room stood to give the risen Jesus a standing ovation!

Brothers and sisters, we are sent people because Jesus won! After all the suffering is over, after all the battles have been fought, after all the dust has settled, Jesus, who was sent by God, is still with us, still in the lead, still sending us out to welcome and advance the kingdom of God. And Jesus will not stop sending people like us until the kingdom comes and God's will is done on earth as it is in heaven.

> **Be filled with the Holy Spirit and embrace a supernatural lifestyle that bears fruit and exposes the kingdom of God.**

And *that* Jesus deserves all our praise, honor, and worship because *that* Jesus is worth it.

Paul said the good news about Jesus is for everyone who believes (Rom. 1:16). The Greek word for *believe* in Romans 1:16 has the same root as the Greek word for *faith*. Getting this word down is a key to everything. This brand of faith is not about accepting a list of facts. And it isn't, as J. D. Walt said, a "kind of lever that we pull in order to make something else happen." That's how you birth heresies. As Walt said, faith is the life of Jesus living itself out in me.[23] It is fellowship with the triune God.

The collective witness and teaching of Scripture tell me that the voice of God can be expected to speak into the lives of those who are fully awake to God's movements on earth. Will you hear the call? Will you go where he sends, taking with you power and authority to cast out demons, cure diseases, proclaim the kingdom, and heal the sick?

LISTENING TO THE WORD

All I want for you at the end of this story is for you to be filled with the Holy Spirit and embrace a supernatural lifestyle that bears fruit and exposes the kingdom of God. If you've done it, send me a note. I will invite my community to pray for you to take authority over your sent-ness. Together, let's welcome God's kingdom on earth as it is in heaven.

Group Gathering

OPEN WITH PRAYER

WATCH SESSION 8 VIDEO

DISCUSS THE FOLLOWING QUESTIONS BASED ON READINGS 36–40

36

Key Observation
This is what it means to be sent. It means bearing fruit. It means recognizing that the kingdom keeps moving and that we are called to move with it, in the footsteps of Jesus, our Apostle and High Priest.

Question for Discussion
How does this call to sent-ness change your understanding of what it means to follow Jesus? And how does sent-ness interact with a call to supernatural ministry?

37

Key Observation
To be an apostolic church is to believe that what we hold has been given to us to carry forward. We have both a call and a commission. We are sent people.

Question for Discussion
How important is it to you that the faith you have is passed along to the next generation? Is that value for you?

38

Key Observation
A testimony defeats the Enemy by changing the spiritual climate. It unleashes possibilities. It unleashes the "do it again" power of the miracle you're witnessing to.

Question for Discussion
Have you considered the idea that your story might have power to create a miracle in someone else's life?

39

Key Observation
Never forget who you are. You are a follower of Jesus who has been given power and authority to cast out all demons, to cure diseases, to proclaim the kingdom of God, and to heal the things that destroy people's lives.

Question for Discussion
How has this study influenced your understanding of what it means to follow Jesus into supernatural ministry?

40

Key Observation
Jesus will not stop sending people like us until the kingdom comes and God's will is done on earth as it is in heaven.

Question for Discussion
Why do you suppose God chooses to partner with people (rather than working around us or in spite of us) in his pursuit of advancing the kingdom on earth?

CLOSE WITH PRAYER

As you move into a closing time of prayer, share stories of how God has changed your worldview through this study. Talk especially about what you've learned about prayer, spiritual warfare, the kingdom of God, healing, or faith. After each person shares, have the group gather around, lay hands on, and pray over that person at the point of their deep need.

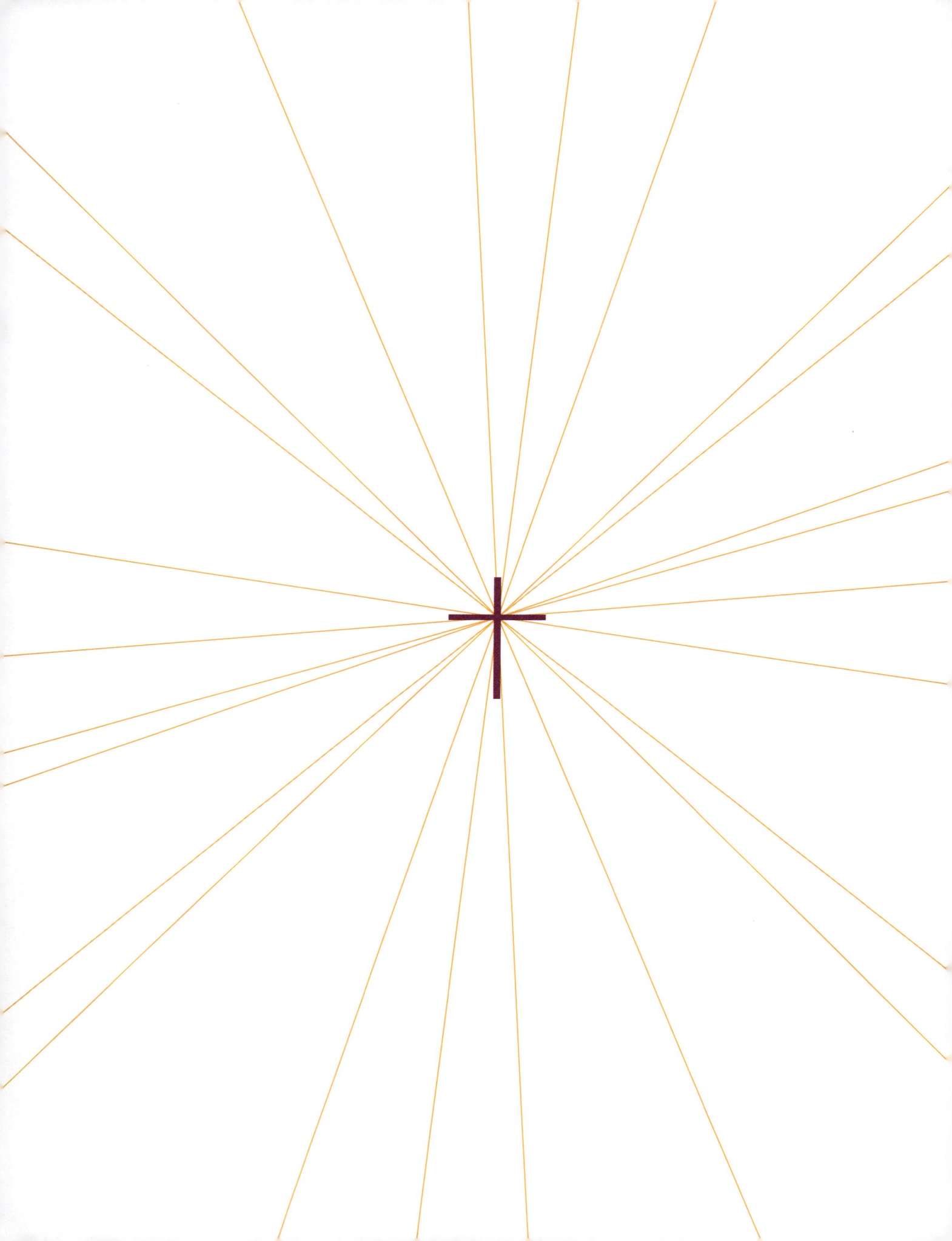

NOTES

1. I stole this line from Mike Pilavachi. He is an evangelist, pastor, and leader of a ministry called Soul Survivor in the UK.
2. C. S. Lewis, *Mere Christianity* (New York: HarperOne, 1952), 134.
3. David Watson, "Remember That Time John Wesley Raised the Dead?" (May 25, 2017), https://www.ministrymatters.com/all/entry/8202/remember-that-time-john-wesley-raised-the-dead.
4. C. S. Lewis, *Mere Christianity* (New York: Touchstone/Simon & Schuster, 1996), 55–56.
5. Henri J. M. Nouwen, *You Are the Beloved: Daily Meditations for Spiritual Living*, comp. and ed. Gabrielle Earnshaw (New York: Convergent, 2017), 247.
6. Thomas Merton, *Conjectures of a Guilty Bystander* (New York: Image Books, 1966), 156.
7. John Wesley, *The Works of the Reverend John Wesley*, ed. John Emory, vol. 4 (New York: B. Waugh and T. Mason, 1835), 49.
8. Thomas Merton, *Conjectures of a Guilty Bystander* (New York: Image Books, 1966), 156.
9. John Wesley, *The Works of the Reverend John Wesley*, ed. John Emory, vol. 4 (New York: B. Waugh and T. Mason, 1835), 282.
10. John Piper, "God Is Always Doing 10,000 Things in Your Life" (January 1, 2013), https://www.desiringgod.org/articles/god-is-always-doing-10000-things-in-your-life.
11. R. T. Kendall, "Why Jack Hayford's Church Grew After He Saw Shekinah Glory," https://www.charismamag.com/spirit/bible-study/40559-rt-kendall-why-jack-hayford-s-church-grew-after-he-saw-shekinah-glory. This article is adapted from *More of God: Seek the Benefactor, Not Just the Benefits* (Charisma House, 2019).
12. Richard Rohr, *A Lever and a Place to Stand: The Contemplative Stance, the Active Prayer* (New York: Paulist Press, 2011), kindle loc 610.
13. Sun Tzu, *The Art of War*, translated with commentary by Lionel Giles (Digireads.com Publishing, 2016), 8.
14. Story shared with permission by Maggie Freitag, student leader at Mosaic Church, in May 2019.
15. Ibid.
16. *The Oxford Dictionary of the Christian Church*, 3rd ed. (Oxford: Oxford University Press, 1997), 10.
17. Colleen Graham, "What Does James Bond Drink?" 5/15/19, https://www.thespruceeats.com/james-bond-drinks-760178.

18. Benjamin Pratt, *Ian Fleming's Seven Deadlier Sins & 007's Moral Compass* (Read the Spirit Books, 2018), kindle loc 472.

19. Sara Bryant, "A. J. Hackett and the History of Bungee Jumping," https://www.talk-business.co.uk/2016/09/22/aj-hackett-history-bungee-jumping/.

20. Mark Buchanan, "Messy, Costly, Dirty Ministry: The Risk of Welcoming Those Nobody Else Wants," *Christianity Today*, https://www.christianitytoday.com/pastors/2009/spring/messycostlydirtyministry.html.

21. Ibid.

22. Uwe Siemon-Netto, "Science, 'Frauds' Trigger a Decline in Atheism," *Washington Times* (March 3, 2005), http://www.washtimes.com/world/20050303-115733-9519r.htm.

23. J. D. Walt, "The Most Important Word in the New Testament" (August 19, 2018), https://www.seedbed.com/important-word-new-testament/.

Also available:

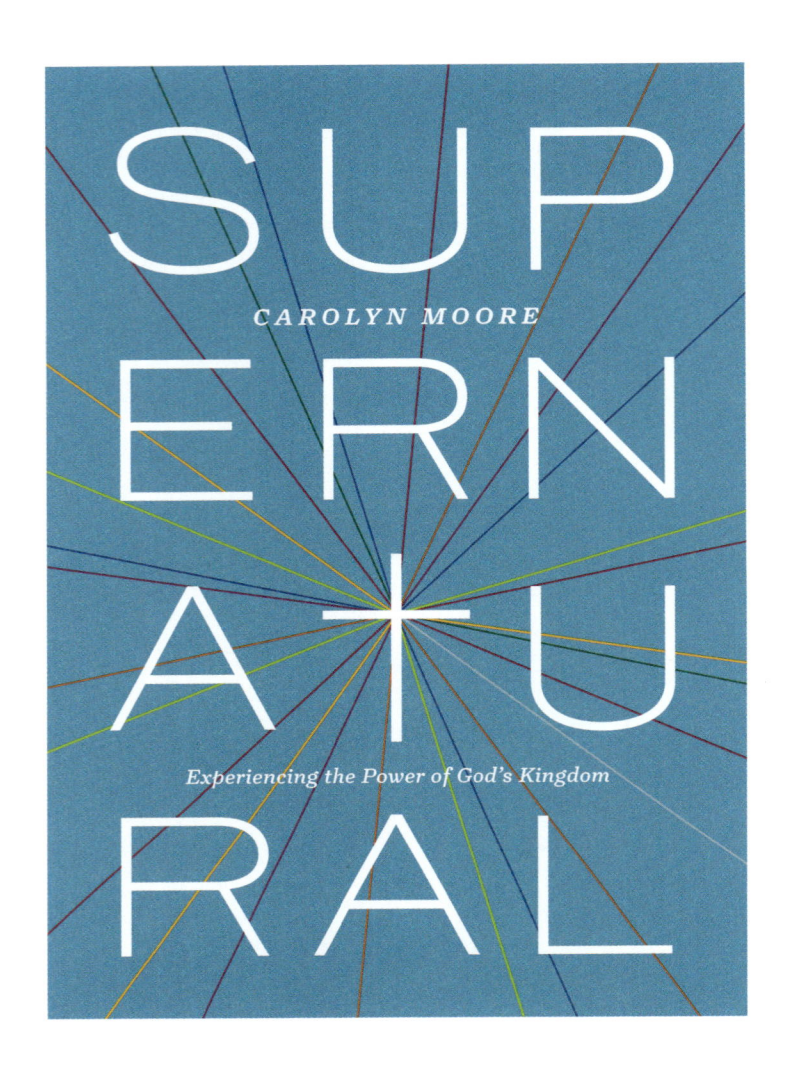

SUPERNATURAL
VIDEO SESSIONS

Eight sessions with Carolyn Moore
available on DVD and/or streaming video.

Seedbed

seedbed.com